A Study Guide for the New Edexcel IGCSE Anthology Non-Fiction Texts for the English Language Exam:
A Line by Line Analysis of all the Extracts with Exam Tips for Success

Josephine Pearce

A Study Smart Guide
© Purley Press 2016

T0018680

Edexcel

International GCSE in English Language
Paper 1 Non-fiction Texts and Transactional Writing
For the Exam

1. The Danger of a Single Story by Chimamanda Ngozi Adichie

2. A Passage to Africa by George Alagiah

3. The Explorer's Daughter by Kari Herbert

4. Explorers or boys messing about? Either way, taxpayer gets rescue bill by Steven Morris

5. Between a Rock and a Hard Place, Aron Ralston

6. Young and dyslexic? You've got it going on by Benjamin Zephaniah

7. A Game of Polo with a Headless Goat, Emma Levine

8. Beyond the Sky and the Earth: A Journey into Bhutan, Jamie Zeppa

9. H is for Hawk, Helen Macdonald

10. Chinese Cinderella, Adeline Yen Mah

Edexcel

International GCSE in English Language

Paper 1 Non-fiction Texts and Transactional Writing

Exam worth 60% of entire IGCSE in English Language

Content of Exam:

Section A: there will be a mixture of short and long-answer questions related to a non-fiction text from **Part 1 of the Anthology** and one previously unseen extract. Questions will focus on the techniques the writer uses.
Worth 30%

Section B: there will be one writing task, based on a choice of two prompts involving a given audience, form or purpose. Worth 30%

This book is a guide to all the non-fiction texts contained in the Part 1: Non-fiction texts section of the Edexcel International GCSE Anthology for Section A of the English Language exam.

Each non-fiction text is analysed in detail, explaining any difficult language, and giving a comprehensive analysis of literary techniques.

The Danger of a Single Story by Chimamanda Ngozi Adichie

Biography

Chimamanda Ngozi Adichie was born in September 1997 in Nigeria, to a father who was a University Professor and a mother who was the University of Nigeria's first female registrar. After studying medicine initially in Nigeria, she moved to the USA and obtained degrees from Yale and Johns Hopkins Universities. Her second novel, "Half of a Yellow Sun", about the Nigerian Civil War, won the Orange Prize, and her poetry and short stories have also been very successful. An extract from another TED talk, "We Should All be Feminists", was sampled in 2013 by Beyoncé Knowles.

Background

Adichie delivers this as a speech at a TED conference. TED stands for "Technology, Education, Design". TED conferences are run by a North American charity which promotes events at which major speakers give short talks, which are then broadcast free and available to all over the internet. Many famous speakers have included Bill Clinton, Al Gore, Bono, and Richard Dawkins. The conferences are a means of spreading interesting ideas, particularly amongst young people. Adichie has chosen to give this speech therefore to reach as many people as possible.

Summary

In this extract Adichie explains how everyone is affected by the stories they tell and the stories they hear. In particular she looks at the way that people judge or interpret others in a very limited way, because they only have a "single story" about a person, due to their race, nationality or social status. Adichie illustrates this with a number of examples. She begins by talking about the way that the first books she read, which were only about white European children, caused her to think this was the way she had to write about the world. She then remembers when, as a middle-class girl with servants, she had only a very stereotyped view of the young village boy who worked as their servant, feeling sorry for him, rather than understanding his life. Adichie then shifts to when she was a student in America, and how her roommate had assumed she came from a very primitive background. She then realises how it would be easy for American students who didn't understand modern Africa to have such a limited view. Adichie then realises that she had been equally wrong in her views about Mexico, before she herself visited. She finishes by discussing a thought by Alice Walker, the famous writer, that stories can have the opposite effect; rather than giving a single story, they can open up the stories of others and gives us a wider and more sympathetic view.

Analysis

The passage starts with a very short sentence, "I'm a storyteller." (Line 1). This statement in the first person immediately grabs our attention, and establishes that Adichie will be talking about herself. It is a very firm and commanding way to open a passage. It also establishes that she will be telling us about stories themselves, and how they are a significant part of her life.

The next sentence starts with "And", which as a conjunction is not usually found in formal written English. However it is very powerful here as it continues with the direct, conversational tone that Adichie sets up with her short opening sentence. She continues to tell us directly that she would like to tell some "personal stories" about herself. She introduces the title of the piece when she says she would like to tell us about the "danger of the single story". She creates a sense of suspense by not defining what the "danger" might be yet. We will clearly have to continue paying attention to what she says.

As this passage is autobiographical – literally writing about oneself – she follows the convention of autobiography by telling us about her early life. She tells us where she grew up – on a University campus, in Nigeria, West Africa. At this point (line 3) she introduces her mother. Adichie tells us that her mother says that Adiche started reading at two, which is a very early age. However Adichie then undercuts this by saying that four is probably "close to the truth". Adichie cleverly introduces two versions of the truth here; there is no "single story" even about something seemingly as personal as when one started reading. The reader is therefore subtly introduced to a further aspect of the title and theme of the piece – that there are many different ways of seeing the world, and one's own memory and opinions cannot be wholly relied upon. She only ever says that she can get "close to the truth" – she never claims she can tell the whole truth. There are always different ways of seeing one event.

The next paragraph (line 6) expands upon the previous one to give us more detail about Adichie's childhood. She began to write stories at the age of seven, in pencil with crayon. She uses the adjective "poor" in connection with her mother to create an amusing picture of her mother having to read these stories, politely, when they are not very good. The paragraph is composed of a single sentence, which has two parts, which balance each other. The first sets up that Adichie is writing stories that her mother, through duty, has to read, and that these stories are based on the ones that the author herself was reading. The second part, after a colon (line 8), lists what the stories she writes are like. Adichie is a very famous black African writer, and the reader who is aware of her ethnicity would be surprised by the description of the stories that she produces. All of the details are European in origin – snow, apples, the surprise of the sun appearing, the main characters being "white and blue-eyed". By dividing the sentence like this, and holding back the details of the story until after the colon, Adichie creates suspense, and accentuates the contrast between the details of her real life in Africa, and the stories she writes. Adichie's next sentence again opens with an intimate and conversational tone, with "Now", which brings us into the world of reality and focuses our attention. Adichie repeats "Nigeria" twice (line 11) to underline the difference between the stories she was writing, and the reality of her home country. She uses the word "mangoes" (line 12) to balance the "apples" of line 9. She also makes gentle fun of the fact that Europeans (in particularly British people) are obsessed with talking about the weather, by saying there was no need to. Nigeria has a consistently warm climate, with little change from season to season, unlike Europe.

After these anecdotes about her early life, Adichie moves in the next paragraph (line 14) to analysing what these experiences might mean. Adichie is very clever in this extract in drawing universal conclusions from the incidents of her own childhood. She talks about the way that everyone, but especially children, is open to be influenced very strongly by the stories that they read, or that they are told. Adichie has only ever read stories which had characters who were "foreign" – namely that they were not Nigerian, but came from other countries. Adichie thought that all books therefore had to have characters who were foreign to her, and who lived lives very different to hers, and who looked very different to her as well. Again, Adichie starts a sentence with "Now" (line 17), to signal that we as readers should pay close attention to what she has to say: "Now, things changed when I discovered African books". This is also another short sentence, following a long sentence that ran over four lines; Adichie uses these short sentences to draw attention to the point she is making. She is precise and concise. She goes on to tell us that these African books are rare, difficult to find, which is why she has not come across them before.

Again, the next paragraph starts with a conjunction, "But" (line 20), as we again get the sense of Adiche speaking directly to us. She quotes the names of two very famous African writers, Chinua Achebe and Camara Laye. Adichie tells us that the discovery of these authors had a massive impact – she uses a metaphor in the word "shift" to describe how she moves from one opinion to another. She realised that there was another way of describing her life, which was more truthful and authentic. To describe herself she uses an image, "skin the colour of chocolate" which is a striking contrast to the "white and blue-eyed" characters of her early stories (line 8). Adichie describes how she has "kinky hair", which is too tightly curled to be put into a pony tail. She realises then that girls who look like her – who are black and African - can also appear in literature.

The words "skin" "colour" "chocolate" and "kinky" use alliteration of the hard "c" or "k" sound to make the reader even more aware of them. They add to the power of the contrast that Adiche is making, between the reality of her life and appearance, and the characters she has read about. Adichie starts the next paragraph again with "Now", because she has not yet finished making her point and is still trying to keep the reader's attention. She tells us (line 24) that she still loved the British and American books that she read, because they were able to introduce to other types of people, westerners who grew up in Europe or North America. She uses two metaphors to tell us this. In a very short sentence she tells us they 'stirred' her imagination – which is an image of vigorous movement, like stirring the water in a cup, or stirring people into action. This means that it changed her, and made her see things differently She then says that books had opened up "new worlds"; this is a metaphor of action and adventure and new experiences and exploration. When European explorers discovered America, they called it the "New World". Adichie means that books are like discovering brand new countries. However, she uses 'But' to start the next sentence (line 25) to tell us that this has had the consequence that she thought they showed the *only* types of people who deserved to be in books. African writers show that there is another way of writing about people, and that very different lives can all be valid and written about. Adichie ends the section by returning to the title of the extract (line 27) and saying that discovering African writers saves her from having a "single story" about books. There are many different people, many different stories, and all of them can be included in books.

After this analysis of the way she came to realise that books can be about many things, Adichie moves to a different way in which a single story can be dangerous. She gives an example from her real life experience to show how we should be careful not to assume we know everything about other people and their lives.

Adichie opens the next paragraph (line 28) with a description of her family life in Nigeria. She comes from a "middle-class" family, with a father who is a professor and a mother who is also a professional, a University administrator. At the age of eight, Adichie's family take in a "house boy", a young child servant who performs domestic duties. His name, "Fide," is Latin for faithful. Adichie's mother does not tell her children anything about his life, only that his family is "very poor". Again this paragraph uses Adichie's technique of starting sentences with "Now" (lines 29, 33) which here serves to grab our attention, and makes the scenes described vivid and present to us. Adichie's mother sends yams (a local vegetable) and rice and old clothes to Fide's family. The paragraph ends with the first example of reported speech in the extract, which further brings the scene to life. The sentence that Adichie's mother says when Adichie doesn't eat her dinner is made even more striking by the use of alliteration of the "f" sounds; Fide's family are so poor, Adichie should eat all her dinner, as she is lucky to be born into a prosperous family and should never waste the advantages that she has.

However there is much more to Fide's life that Adichie has been led to believe in her mother's simplistic view. Adichie recounts (line 36) an actual visit to Fide's village, where Fide's mother shows her a beautiful basket made of "dyed raffia" – a brightly coloured thick twine. Adichie's amazement is clear in the very short sentence (lines 36-7) "I was startled". Adichie has only had one possible story about Fide's family – they were poor – and as such she could not even imagine it was possible that they could have colour and beauty and creativity in their lives. Adichie sums this up in the final sentence of this paragraph: "Their poverty was my single story of them".

In the next two paragraphs, Adichie moves us forward in time, to when she is a 19-year old student in a university in the United States of America. Adichie very cleverly shows us what happens when she is in the position that Fide was. Adichie's American roommate has a very limited stereotype of Africans. The roommate is "shocked by her" (line 44) and makes assumptions about Adichie's life. Adichie's roommate cannot understand why Adichie can speak English so well, and is "confused" when she is told that Nigeria's official language is English. The roommate believes that all Africans must listen to "tribal music". The fact that Adichie puts this in speech marks makes it comic – we can imagine the roommate saying this, and we can imagine the disappointment she feels when Adichie produces a tape by the American singer Mariah Carey.

The roommate believes that Adichie "did not know how to use a stove" (line 48). This is funny because we have already learned that Adichie comes from a prosperous family. Adichie just lets the single sentence stand alone as a paragraph, without comment, to add to its impact.

Adichie in the next paragraph comments on this comic story to bring out the deeper moral point. She starts with a clear personal statement: "What struck me was this" (line 49). The word "struck" is a metaphor of force or violence, which brings out how deeply Adichie was affected and upset by this encounter.

Her roommate could not see her clearly, because she already had a "single story" about Adichie. Adichie's unhappiness at this way of being treated is very firmly expressed in the hard "p" sounds of "patronizing", "pity" and "no possibility" (lines 51-53). The roommate has "a single story of Africa: a single story of catastrophe". This cleverly balanced phrase, with a colon at the centre, shows how for the American roommate, "Africa" and "catastrophe" have become synonymous or the same. The identical "a" "f" and "ph" sounds in "Africa" and "catastrophe" further show how the two ideas have become one in the roommate's mind. By defining Africa as catastrophe, which means a terrible disaster or crisis, we see that the roommate has heard only negative stories of famine, disease or war, for example.

The repetition, three times, of the phrase "no possibility" at the end of the passage shows the depth of Adichie's emotion as she realises that the "single story" that the roommate has means there can never be a "connection as human equals". Adichie will always be seen as different. Adichie is too clever to think that she herself cannot make the same mistakes as her American roommate. She moves her account of her life on a number of years (line 54), and tells us that after a time spent living in the United States she understands why her college roommate might have developed a one-sided view. This is because the only images of Africa that most people see in the Western media are very limited. Adichie contrasts a place of "beautiful landscapes" and "beautiful animals" (lines 56 and 57) with "incomprehensible people, fighting senseless wars" who are dying of "poverty and AIDS". These are extreme images; either things are very beautiful, or very violent and negative. Things are never just normal. Adichie skilfully builds up to a climax in this long sentence (lines 55-59), culminating with the image of Africans waiting for a "kind, white foreigner" to save them. This is very much the image that we might remember from appeals from charities in the media, which use emotive pictures of poor people in Africa to raise funds.

Adichie finishes this paragraph by reintroducing Fide (lines 59-60); just as a prosperous African family had made assumptions about Fide's family, so Adichie herself now finds herself looking back on Africa itself in the same way. "I would see Africans in the same way that I, as a child, had seen Fide's family".

In the next paragraph, Adichie uses the phrase "I must quickly add", which creates a sense of urgency as she reveals she is "just as guilty in the question of the single story" (line 61). This creates a sense of trust in the reader; Adichie lets us know what she thinks, even if it is unpleasant, which might in turn encourage us as readers to be honest.

Adichie again uses a personal story to make a wider point. She has visited Mexico from the US. At the time of the visit, politicians in the United States were discussing immigration, and the situation was "tense". Much as Africa had been associated both with beautiful landscapes and terrible poverty in the mind of most Americans, its neighbour Mexico had also become a single story: "immigration became synonymous with Mexicans" (line 64). Adichie uses hyperbole or overstatement here, and emotive language. There are "endless" stories of Mexicans "fleecing the healthcare system" or "sneaking across the border" or being "arrested at the border". This negative language like "fleecing" or "sneaking" and "arrested" shows how negatively Mexicans are seen by certain Americans.

She also ends the paragraph with a humorous and throwaway line "that sort of thing". This is understatement, which gives a comic tone to what Adichie is saying. It also briefly makes it seem that Adichie is sympathising or agreeing with these prejudices.

However, this comic tone contrasts strongly with the very serious point Adichie makes in the next paragraph (line 67 onwards). Once she arrives in Guadalajara, a town in Mexico, she has the same experience she went through as a child, when she met Fide's family and realised that she had a very one-sided view. Adichie stresses the importance of direct personal experience by repeating "I remember" in lines 67 and 68. She introduces a series of vivid images of what she saw in Mexico. She describes working people "rolling up tortillas in the marketplace, smoking, laughing". The repeated present participles (verbs ending in "ing") create a sense of constant activity. She moves from "slight surprise" to a much stronger emotion, which she introduces with one of her very effective short sentences: "And then, I was overwhelmed with shame" (line 69). She realises that she herself has been guilty of seeing Mexicans as "one thing", the "abject immigrant". She has "bought into the single story of Mexicans" and this realisation causes her great emotional distress. Adichie bravely tells us this: "I could not have been more ashamed of myself" (line 72).

Adichie sums up her analysis of the meaning of "single story" in her next short paragraph. Again she starts with a short word "so" to catch the reader's attention. Then she uses repetition to strong effect to make her point that a "single story" about a whole people or country arises when they are shown as "one thing, as only one thing, over and over again" (lines 73-74). After showing the "danger of a single story", Adichie chooses literary techniques to emphasise that stories can be a powerful force for good. She does this by moving from the singular noun to the plural; from "a single story" to "Stories matter" (line 75). This is a very short sentence – the shortest sentence possible, being a subject and verb only. She follows it up with another very short sentence, adding only odd words: "Many stories matter". This powerfully emphasises the word "many", in opposition to the word "single". She also starts the next two sentences with the plural noun "stories".

Adichie compares and contrasts stories which "dispossess" and are "malign" with other stories which can "empower" and "humanize". She uses two metaphors which are opposite in meaning in the final sentence of this paragraph (lines 76 and 77), when she says that stories can "break the dignity" of a people, but can also "repair that broken dignity". The dignity of a people is likened to a precious object that can be broken by some stories, but repaired by the power of other stories that are told. She is doing this to tell us that stories have a great power to heal.

Adichie introduces a quotation from the famous African-American writer, Alice Walker, whose novel "The Color Purple" tells us about the difficult lives of Black women in the 1930s in the USA. Walker tells a personal story about her relatives from the South of the United States who had to move to the North. Walker gave them a book about their former life and in reading this book "a kind of paradise was regained". Paradise is another word for heaven. This is also an allusion to "Paradise Regained", a poem by John Milton from 1671, which is a sequel to his famous "Paradise Lost", about Adam and Eve being forced from heaven by God. Adichie reminds us that books have a power that lasts a long time, and that whatever one has lost in one's life, imagination can bring it back.

Adichie (line 84) uses the word "paradise" again in her concluding paragraph. She brings back also the title of the piece by reminding us that there is never a "single story" about any place or thing, and that when we realise that there are many different ways of seeing the world, we get back a "kind of paradise".

A Passage to Africa by George Alagiah

Biography

George Alagiah was born in Sri Lanka in 1955, and moved to Ghana as a child in 1961. Educated at Durham University, he was a print journalist before joining the BBC in 1989, and travelling around the world as a foreign correspondent, in many dangerous areas, including Rwanda, Iraq and Afghanistan. More recently he has worked as a newsreader for the BBC on its main evening programmes.

Background

The book "A Passage to Africa" looks at a number of countries in Africa, through Alagiah's work there as a journalist, as well as memories of his time there as a child. Somalia is the focus of this extract. It is a mainly Islamic country in the Horn of Africa, which obtained independence after World War Two, after decades of Italian and British colonial rule. In 1991, the revolutionary government which had ruled since 1969 was overthrown by violent factions fighting for control, displacing millions of people and leading to a catastrophic famine.

Summary

Between 1991 and 1992 Alagiah visited Somalia, which was terribly affected by famine and war. This extract talks about the incidents of a single day, and a memorable but brief encounter with a local man. Alagiah is driven to a very remote village, and comes across a number of very sick and dying people. Alagiah explains throughout this extract that journalists become hardened to the scenes of suffering they come across; they are almost callous in their search for more and more shocking images. Alagiah describes people suffering from awful wounds, and dwells upon a number of upsetting details. He emphasises that the people are trying always to preserve their dignity. He finally makes eye contact briefly with a man who smiles at him; the translator explains that the man has smiled because he is embarrassed to be seen in such a poor condition. This upsets Alagiah, and he can no longer be so composed or passive in his attitude to suffering. This one look has stayed with him throughout the intervening years, although he never found out the man's name; it humanises the suffering he reports upon, and reminds Alagiah not to become too callous in search of a story.

Analysis

Alagiah opens with a short sentence in the first person. The simple past tense verb "I saw" establishes that the passage will be based on his own experience. He then tells us he saw "a thousand hungry, lean, scared and betrayed faces" as he "criss-crossed Somalia" in East Africa in 1991 and 1992. Alagiah is cleverly using a very long list of negative adjectives, and the hyperbole in the use of a very large number of people, to contrast with the way that a single face of an African had a massive impact upon him, and continues to have an impact in the present day: "there is one I will never forget". Moving from the past to the future tense alerts us to the fact that what Alagiah encountered in that one face was permanent and life-changing for him.

Alagiah (line 3) then plunges us into the narrative directly. The use of the phrases "little hamlet", or tiny village, and the dismissive "back of beyond" make us perhaps underestimate the impact that location and events there will have. The village of Gufgadud and surrounding places have not yet been visited by Aid Agencies. Alagiah quotes his own notebook of the time for instructions, and everything seems very normal and matter-of-fact, just like road directions would be in our everyday lives (lines 5-6). However, Alagiah introduces a startling adjective. The hamlet is "like a ghost village". A ghost town is a town with no inhabitants. This image is one of abandonment, but also might alert us to the presence of death.

Line 8 continues supernatural imagery with the use of "ghoulish" to describe his own profession – journalists "on the hunt" for striking pictures. The real meaning of Ghoul is a creature from Arab mythology that lives on dead human flesh. The implication here is that journalists seek out and feed on human misery in order to get stories. Already (lines 9 -10), what would have "appalled" Alagiah and his colleague a few days ago "no longer impressed us much". Alagiah explains that the "search for the shocking is like the craving for a drug". This simile means that journalists are so interested in funding new and shocking stories, it is like a drug addict who continually wants their drug and needs larger and larger doses; journalists are constantly looking for increasingly awful events.

This is a terrible admission to make and must affect the reader's view of reporters and their morality. Alagiah uses alliteration of the "s" sound to link the "search for the shocking" with the everyday words "same old stuff". This shows us that what was once shocking is now thought normal, "just a fact of life". He tells us that although it seems "callous", this is how journalists create moving images for people in the "comfort of their living rooms". Alagiah uses everyday phrases – even clichés – like this to contrast the awful things he says with the comfort of our normal lives in the West. He does this to shock us out of our complacency.

The next two paragraphs (line 16, and line 24) both start with "There was", confronting us with reality, and descriptions of real events, not just his opinion. He introduces by name a local woman Aminda Abdirahman, and in using her name makes her more real and human to the reader. Amina had gone out to look for roots to eat, leaving her two daughters lying on the "dirt floor" of the hut. After the use of ghost" and "ghoulish", we get the next image of death. Habiba, aged ten, and her sister Ayaan, nine, are "reaching the final, enervating stage of terminal hunger". This means that they are literally dying of hunger.

The next sentence is a euphemism – when a writer cannot bring themselves to say something directly, because it is too shocking: "By the time Amina returned, she had only one daughter." Then Alagiah hits us with the brutal truth: "Habiba had died." The next sentence lacks a main verb, which gives it an incomplete or unfinished quality, and adds to the reader's discomfort as Alagiah describes the way in which Habiba dies. She does not "rage" at dying, there is no "whimpering". She passes away in a "simple, frictionless, motionless deliverance". She was already in a state of "half-life".

The phrase "half-life" is usually used in science to describe levels of radiation, but Alagiah is making a new metaphor here: he means that Habiba was half-alive and half-dead, unable to be saved by any doctor. Alagiah uses these strange adjectives to try to talk about what is very upsetting, and to paint a scene in which Habiba was already so weak and immobile that her death was almost imperceptible.

The next paragraph (line 24) introduces another victim, this time nameless. She is an "old woman" who has been "abandoned by relatives". Alagiah stresses the awful nature of the scene by repeating the words "the smell": he is overwhelmed by the stench of "decaying flesh". Alagiah gives a succession of horrifying images. He notes that a wound on her shin is the size of his hand – giving us a comparison we can relate to. What is most shocking is that her leg has been bent out of shape. He describes this using a metaphor – the leg has "fused into the gentle V-shape of a boomerang". The word "gentle" is unexpected in such a terrible scene. We are used to thinking of a boomerang as a toy, but it is also a hunting weapon of the Australian aboriginal population – again this links to the fact that searching for food in an extreme climate is now a fact of life in Somalia.

The next sentence (line 29) is very short, and makes it clear that the old lady and her wound have become one in the mind of the narrator: "It was rotting, she was rotting". Alagiah uses sibilance of the "s" sound again in "sick, yellow eyes", "smell" and "struggling breath" as he describes her terrible state (lines 29-31). This is also an example of onomatopoeia, as the "s" sound is like someone dying and struggling for air. This brings the awful scene closer for the reader.

The next paragraph (line 33) is a single sentence. Alagiah repeats the words from his opening sentence, as he introduces the main theme of this passage: "And then there was the face I will never forget". The reader will therefore think they are getting to the heart of the passage and its message.

However, Alagiah delays introducing a description of this face, and instead introduces a digression. He analyses the way that people react to human misery. Alagiah tells us that his reaction to everyone he met that day (line 34) is a mixture of "pity and revulsion" – disgust at what he sees. He repeats this, in the next sentence, which lacks a main verb, as if Alagiah is trying breathlessly to convince a reader who does not believe him: "Yes, revulsion". Alagiah goes on to use nightmarish imagery. He personifies "hunger and disease" as "twin evils" who, like a vampire, suck the human body of its "natural vitality" or life force. This is "disgusting", a fact which he admits is never said in television reports. He calls this a "taboo" (line 36) which means something that society cannot accept or even talk about.

Alagiah starts the next two sentences (line 36 and 37) with the same phrase "To be in a feeding centre". He does this to bring us to the heart of the action, and he admits feeling and doing things in the face of human suffering that do not reflect well upon him. He describes a "feeding centre" where the starving people cannot control their bowels, and he tells us how he can "hear and smell the excretion of fluids". He then admits that he "surreptitiously" or secretly wipes his hands on his trousers after holding the hand of a mother who has "just cleaned vomit from her child's mouth". Alagiah is trying to be very honest about his feelings here; although he feels sorry for the people, he cannot help feeling disgusted by their illness.

Alagiah starts the next paragraph by returning to "pity" (line 41) after the descriptions of the revulsion he felt above. He tells us that the people struggle to retain human dignity in such a terrible situation. He describes how an old woman will cover her "shrivelled" body with a "soiled cloth" (line 45). He echoes the word "soiled" in the next image, in which he talks about a dying man who keeps his "hoe" or gardening tool next to him, as if means to go out an "till the soil". There is a grim irony in the fact that he is lying next to a mat that will one day "shroud his corpse" (line 44). Life and death are so close to each here other they cannot be easily disentangled. This is why it is a "ghost village".

Alagiah's digression is over. The next paragraph suddenly brings us to the face that Alagiah will never forget (line 46). He only saw it for a "few seconds". He uses internal rhyme to accentuate the impact of this sight. It is a "fleeting meeting of eyes" before the person disappears into the "darkness" of the hut. He repeats the word "smile" three times in one sentence, and tries to understand using abstract nouns what the smile means. It is not a "smile of greeting" or a "smile of joy"; Alagiah uses a rhetorical question "how could it be?" in an aside to the reader to signal his puzzlement, as he tells us that the smile "touched me in a way a could not explain". It goes beyond the two emotions he has just described, of "pity and revulsion" (line 51).

Alagiah uses a rhetorical question again (line 52), opening a paragraph with this uncertainty: "What was it about that smile"? Such rhetorical questions she he has no answer. Alagiah uses a very short sentence "I had to find out" to show his urgency here. The translator asks the man, and we have a brief passage of reported speech as we learn that the man "was embarrassed to be found in this condition". Again, Alagiah introduces a short sentence, which opens unusually with a conjunction: "And then it clicked". This is a metaphor of a light coming on, or things falling into place, which expresses how suddenly Alagiah has understood what the man meant. It is the "feeble smile" (line 55) that someone gives if they are sorry about something or feel like they are guilty of doing "something wrong" (line 56).

Alagiah's next paragraph tells us that he is normally hardened or "inured" to such "stories of suffering", a phrase made stronger by the alliteration. Alagiah then gives us an analysis of the normal relationship between journalist and subject of his or her reports. He tells us that journalists are "active" while subjects are "passive": journalists observe only, while the subjects cannot have an influence upon the journalist. Alagiah uses a common, well-used short phrase to explain the impact of this man's smile. It has "turned the tables" (line 61), a metaphor from the game of backgammon. To turn the tables is to suddenly find yourself in the position of the other player, which might not be to your advantage. The man who smiled at Alagiah somehow makes Alagiah consider whether what he is doing as a journalist is right.

Alagiah now looks at himself in the same way he would look at others. This reversal is so powerful that Alagiah uses the violent metaphor that it "cuts to the heart of the relationship" between Alagiah and the poor man, to the whole relationship between the rich western world and the poorer third world: "between us and them, between the rich world and the poor world". The violent metaphor of cut to the heart – or get to the most important part – also reflects the fact that the famine has been caused by violent conflict. The final sentence of this paragraph is another rhetorical question, presumably the very "question" posed by the man's smile (line 62): "If he was embarrassed to be found weakened by hunger and ground down by conflict, how should I feel to be standing there so strong and confident?"

The next short paragraph is Alagiah's answer to this question, which is to continue with his journalistic mission. He is "resolved" to write the story of the town of Gufgaduud with all the "power and purposes I could muster". The word "muster" has a military overtone of gathering forces, which reinforces the strong impact of the "p" alliteration earlier in the line. This military image is very effective, given that the terrible famine has be caused by war, and shows that Alagiah feels he will need all of his strength to write such a story. The next sentence (line 67-8) brings us from the past to the present. It seemed then, "and still does" that Alagiah's only answer to the unspoken question of the man is carry on reporting well.

Alagiah's final paragraph brings this passage to a conclusion, with a revelation about Alagiah's "brief encounter" in Gufgaduud. He has "one regret" about that meeting – that he never learns the man's name. Again, as in the previous paragraph, we are brought back into the present day as Alagiah tells us he has searched through his notes and the original BBC broadcast to find the man's name. Meeting the nameless man – whom he calls his "nameless friend" had a profound and last experience, being a "seminal moment" – a metaphor from the natural world – in that it plants the seed in him for a new understanding of the world. The word seminal literally means relating to seeds.

Meeting the nameless man forms a massive part of the way that Alagiah sees the world, which Alagiah sums up as "the gradual collection of experience we call context". He means here that everything that happens to a person contributes to the way they look at things. Alagiah (lines 73-74) gives a very balanced pair of sentences which sets out a central theme of journalism: "Facts and figures are the easy part of journalism. Knowing where they sit in the great scheme of things is much harder". The encounter with the man with the unforgettable smile has given Alagiah the ability to be a better journalist.

Alagiah thanks the man with a colloquial expression, which you might use with your close friends in a social context: "So, my nameless friend, if you are still alive, I owe you one". "Nameless friend" is an oxymoron or contradiction in terms – how can someone you don't know be your friend? The phrase "I owe you one" usually means that someone is offering to buy you a drink, but here the meaning is also one which reverses the usual relationship of the powerful West and the developing world. Instead of the poor nation being in the rich nation's debt, we have the western journalist in the debt of the poor nameless man.

The Explorer's Daughter by Kari Herbert

Biography

Kari Herbert was born in 1970, the daughter of Sir Wally Herbert, the Polar explorer. She was brought up for the first few years of her life in North Greenland, speaking the local language. She has written for a number of magazines as a travel writer, and in 2005 published "The Explorer's Daughter", her best-known Book. She has made a number of television programmes on themes of exploration and conservation, and is a fellow of the Royal Geographical Society.

Background

Greenland, where the extract takes place, is a large island near the North Pole. First colonised by Vikings, since the 13th century the majority of the population have been Inughuit or the native peoples of the North Pole. The country is mainly self-governing, but still part of the Danish realm, and the head of state is the Danish monarch.

Summary

The events of this extract take place in 2002 during a hunt for narwhal or toothed whale, which the narrator observes from the shore near Thule, a small town in Northern Greenland. She describes the first sighting of two large groups of narwhal in the fjord or inlet, and then the approach of the indigenous people (the Inughuit) to the whale. Herbert intersperses the description of the hunt, seen from a distance, with information about the importance of the narwhal to the Inughuit way of life. Herbert also gives information about the narwhal's life as well. She is careful to put the hunting into context – this is not being done for sport, but for survival – though she has sympathy for the creatures.

Analysis

Herbert opens the passage at a very specific moment in time: "Two hours after the last of the hunters had returned and eaten". Then she introduces the narwhal, who are sighted "this time very close" (line 2). We can presume that before this passage the narwhal were sighted very far away. Herbert then lets us know where she, as narrator and participant in the action of the scene, is standing. She is amongst those people still on shore. These observers can see the whales "with the naked eye". What the observers can see is described in magical imagery. She tells us that she can see the narwhal send up "plumes of spray" which catch the light in a "spectral play of colour" (line 3). The intensity of the experience is expressed though the rhymes of "spray and play" and the repeated "s" and "p" alliteration. "Spectral" is an adjective which means like a ghost. Here it makes the narwhals' arrival seem supernatural or extraordinary, and hints that what we have described is a matter of life and death.

Herbert continues with more visual description. She introduces two large "pods" or groups of whales (line 4) circling in the fjord, or deep sided inlet. She uses two adverbs together to describe how the pods pass by each other "slowly, methodically". Stressing the slowness increases tension in the reader, and gives a sense of suspense. Herbert runs up the hill and again uses a visual adjective to describe the scene's beauty. It is a "glittering kingdom" (line 6). The word kingdom has a connotation of majesty – the whales are majestic creatures, but this also might relate to the very brave hunters. Herbert is moved very deeply by this scene, she takes a "sharp intake of breath". At this distance the hunters are very small, "dotted all around the fjord" (line 7).

Herbert quite often uses compound adjectives in this passage, joining them together with a hyphen. This makes the visual images very intense. The evening light in the fjord is "butter-gold", and it is "glinting off man and whale", linking humankind with the whales, linking hunter and hunted together. It also echoes the "glittering kingdom" described above. Herbert uses alliteration also to highlight the visual descriptions of "soft billows of smoke" from the hunters' pipes. "Billows" is a word mostly used with sails, and it means when a sail fills with the wind. The smoke moves like sails do in the breeze, this metaphor accentuating the maritime theme of the passage, and reminding us the focus of this passage is a battle on the water.

From the lookout Herbert can see the narwhals and the hunters in the distance. They are so close it looks as if "the hunters were close enough to touch the narwhal with their bare hands" but they do not move. This is because distances "can be deceptive" (line 11) in the Arctic region. Herbert finishes with another description which emphasises both the majesty and the mystery of the sight. She wonders whether the narwhal really exist or are "mischievous tricks of the shifting light". The use of the word "mischievous" means that the light itself is personified. Again, this makes the scene appear magical, and that nature itself is a living person.

Herbert's next paragraph (lines 13-16) is much shorter than the second, and very different in tone. This, and the longer following paragraph (lines 17-32) are factual, rather than descriptive and personal, and seek to give a context for the struggle between man and whale that Herbert is witnessing. They are mostly in the present tense, rather than the past tense of the narrative. Herbert tells us that the Narwhal rarely move from the "High Arctic waters", meaning that they stay very close to the North Pole. They only move down to the "slightly more temperate" or warmer waters round the Arctic Circle in the "dead of winter" (lines 13-14). This expression means the middle of winter, but the use of the word "dead" here reminds us that for the narwhal and the Inughuit people there is a battle of life and death, for the Inughuit must kill to survive. In summer – which is when the passage must be set – the narwhal return to the Inglefield Fjord, which is where Herbert is watching the hunt unfold.

Herbert continues to describe the relationship between the narwhal and the Inughuit. She is establishing in terms of nutrition and economics what the narwhal mean. This whole paragraph is written in the third person, and tries to give us information as simply and clearly as possible, as if it were a textbook or magazine report. Herbert is trying to persuade the reader in a rational manner that the hunting is not for sport, but a necessity for survival.

We learn (line 17) that the narwhal is an "essential contributor" to the hunters' survival. Its "mattak" or blubber (a type of fat) contains minerals and nutrients and the high vitamin C content protects the Inughuit against scurvy, which is a painful disease. This disease might arise because it is impossible to grow fruit and vegetables in the cold environment of North Greenland.

Herbert writes about the history of the relationship between people and the whales. The blubber of the whales "for centuries" was the "only source of light and heat" for the Inughuit people. The harsh, barren nature of the snowy landscape is contrasted with the "dark rich meat" of the whales, which is a "valuable" part still of the daily diet for men and dogs. These dogs would be huskies, a key means of transport. In a pair of parentheses Herbert hints at the vast size and value of the whales, as a single narwhal can "feed a team of dogs for an entire month".

Herbert continues to write about the natural history of the narwhal (line 23). She describes how it has a "single ivory tusk" or long tooth, which can grow up to six feet in length (1.75 metres), and in a long sentence she gives a list of all the things for which it can be used by the Inughuit. It is used for "harpoon tips and handles for other hunting implements", the "h" sounds here alerting the reader that all of these uses are linked and related to the action of this extract, which is of course the hunting party in the fjord. Herbert again uses brackets or parentheses to give us extra information, much as she did with the information about the nutritional value of the whale, when she tells us the ivory was too brittle or weak and therefore "not hugely satisfactory as a weapon". This is typical of a more academic or scientific type of writing, which tries to be as precise as possible.

Herbert introduces again an image related to wonder or enchantment (line 26) when she mentions that the tusk could be used to carve a "tupilak" or figure with magical properties; she contrasts this with an eminently more practical use, for the central beam of Inughuit dwellings in the past . Herbert therefore has demonstrated how the narwhal is in every part of Inughuit life, from food, tools, housing, even their magical ceremonies.

Herbert grabs our attention mid-paragraph (line 27) by starting a sentence with "strangely", and then moves from man to the narwhal itself, and what they use their tusks for. This brings us back to a central part of her theme; that human and whale are bound together. We have had a human focus and now it is the whale's turn. The narwhal have little practical use for their own tusks which are not strong enough (line 28) to break through ice to create a breathing hole, nor can they be used to "catch or attack prey". Instead they are used to "disturb the top of the sea bed" to catch Arctic halibut. Herbert then uses a curious phrase which sounds very old-fashioned and perhaps even comic. The narwhal have a "particular predilection" or a strong liking for the fish they are trying to catch. This makes the narwhal seem like they have a character of their own to which we can relate. Herbert then concludes her paragraph with another matter-of-fact statement, which is back to being very impersonal and precise: "Often the ends of their tusks are worn down or even broken from such usage" (line 32).

The next paragraph shifts from the present tense back to a simple past tense, as we return to the narrative of the hunt in the fjord. Herbert uses a verb which is also visual and strongly descriptive. Women are "clustered" on the knoll or small hill of the lookout. Herbert then uses a series of present participles to give a sense of frenzied, ongoing activity. The local women have binoculars "pointing" everywhere, women are "focusing" on their family and "occasionally spinning" when they see the hunters near a narwhal (lines 33-35).

Herbert continues to focus the narrative upon the women waiting on shore. The next clause she introduces (lines 35-36) has a balanced structure which links the women with their husbands, in spite of the distance. Each "wife knew her husband instinctively" and "watched their [the husbands'] progress intently". Herbert uses assonance here to make us focus ourselves on the scene with the same intensity as the wives do. In line 37 we learn the importance of this encounter to the survival of the Inughuit. The narwhal is not only part of the "staple diet" or basic food, but the blubber and meat can be sold to other hunters to bring in extra income. Herbert follows this long sentence with a striking short sentence in order to bring the reader's attention back to the scene on the fjord: "Every hunter was on the water" (line 39). Herbert then uses a pair of similes to zoom out and give us a sense of everything that she sees: "It was like watching a vast, waterborne game with the hunters spread out like a net around the sound". However, the use of the word "game" is deliberately jarring or out-of-place here: this is a matter of life and death, not a game.

Herbert finishes this paragraph by accentuating the stillness of the scene, giving us again some facts about the narwhal that also might make us more sympathetic to the plight of the whales. The narwhal are "intelligent creatures" with keen senses. They can talk to each other under the water, and can hear hunters paddling their kayaks. This is why the hunters must sit "so very still" in the water (line 44).

The next paragraph (lines 45-51) focuses us to one single battle upon the waters. One hunter is "almost on top of a pair of narwhal". The whales themselves are "huge" (line 45). Herbert uses the adverb "gently" to describe the way in which the hunter picks up his harpoon and aims. This word appears to contrast with the potential violence of the action, but it tells us that the hunter is not doing this out of sport, or out of hatred. He is only hunting because he has to, and he has respect for the whale. After the word "aimed", Herbert uses a long dash – which serves to slow the reader down. It is as if time has paused, and we are in a "split second" when Herbert's "heart leapt for both hunter and narwhal". We never find out whether the hunter threw his harpoon. Herbert instead tells us how she is torn between her sympathies for the man, and her sympathies for the whales. Firstly she "urged the man on" (line 47), because he is "so brave to attempt what we was about to do". Herbert then introduces another long dash after these lines – again she pauses the reader, and we are still in the split second before the harpoon is thrown. She reminds us that the hunter is alone, "miles from land in a flimsy kayak" and could drown. He has no rifle, only a harpoon with two heads, and a bladder to keep it afloat once it is thrown, and show where the whale is.

Herbert knows that the hunter is undertaking a "foolhardy exercise" and she respects his bravery. But "at the same time" her "heart" is with the narwhal and she wants it to live. She finishes the paragraph with a series of urgent verbs in the infinitive form. She wants the whale "to dive, to leave, to survive". The strength of her emotions comes out in the rhyme of "dive" and "survive" and the "v" alliteration in all three words. The final word, "survive", is the very heart of this passage. The whale and man are locked in a battle to survive in the harsh High Arctic. The fact that the verbs are in the infinitive form means they are neither past, present, nor future. Herbert is cleverly leaving this battle frozen in time, and we can use our imagination to decide who, if anyone, is the winner. She also implies that the battle between hunter and the hunted is eternal, a changeless part of life.

The final paragraph moves us forward in time. Herbert is now observing from a distance. She does this (line 52) by moving immediately to the simple past tense, which is used for a completed action in the past. She tells us that the "dilemma" stayed with her during the whole of her time living in Greenland. Herbert then moves to the present tense, which signals that this paragraph will be full of informational language, rather than description: "I understand the harshness of life in the Arctic and the needs of the hunters and their families to hunt" (lines 53-54). However, the animals that they hunt are those that "we demand to be protected because of their beauty" (lines 54-55). This is the very "dilemma" that she mentioned earlier; she can understand both sides of the argument. She recognises in a short and powerful sentence the plight of the Inughuit, as well as the fact that our emotional response to hunting might not be right: "And I know that one cannot afford to be sentimental in the Arctic". The word "afford" here has connotations of money, of wealth; the Inughuit literally cannot afford to survive without their hunting. By using the rarely-used impersonal pronoun "one" she is trying to argue that this is a truth, not simply her own opinion.

Herbert introduces a rhetorical question: "How can you possibly eat seal?" which she says she is asked "over and over again" (line 55). Herbert never answers this, but she spends the rest of the paragraph justifying the choices that the Inughuit make. She does this by analysing in detail the economic circumstances of Inughuit life. She starts a sentence with the word "True" which is a concession to the argument that hunting is cruel. She argues though that we have been "bombarded" with images of violent, cruel seal-hunting. The word "bombarded" is a violent metaphor of warfare, of being bombed, and she uses this to alert us to the fact we may have been emotionally manipulated by these terrible pictures. The Inughuit do not "kill for sport" or use the method of clubbing seals to death. They "use every part" of the animals they kill and indeed most of the food they eat they hunt themselves. Herbert repeats the word "kill" three times to illustrate she is not shying away from reality here.

Herbert sets out very clearly in the next sentence what the true economic situation is (lines 60-64). Imported goods are scarce, and there is only an annual supply ship that can break through the ice to reach their home at Qaanaaq, and a small plane from West Greenland can only come twice a week. Herbert finishes the extract with a very clear short sentence, which leaves no room for doubt about her opinion: "Hunting is still an absolute necessity in Thule" (line 64).

Explorers or boys messing about? Either way, taxpayer gets rescue bill by Steven Morris

Biography

Steven Morris is a journalist for the newspaper *The Guardian*. Before becoming a journalist, he studied at Bath Spa University.

Background

This story is published in *The Guardian*, formerly *The Manchester Guardian*. It is a daily British newspaper, with a reputation of a left-wing or liberal viewpoint. It is owned by a trust, rather than an individual, which was set up in 1936 to try and ensure it could remain free from interference.

Summary

This extract from a newspaper article describes the ill-fated attempt of two British explorers to fly by helicopter to Antarctica. The article describes the incidents as they unfold, as the men ditch in the sea and are picked up by a Chilean naval vessel, with a British ship also attempting to rescue them. The article describes the men's background, and previous unsuccessful attempts at exploration. In particular, the two men's failed attempt to cross to Russia via the Bering Strait in an amphibious vehicle is mentioned. The article quotes a number of sources to comment on the explorers, from one of their wives, to military aviation experts, to an unnamed British government spokesperson. Throughout the extract there are a lot of hints that the men have been ill-prepared and foolish in their attempt, and some attempts at finding humour in their actions.

Analysis

As this is a newspaper article, all of the paragraphs are very short, often made up of a single sentence. This is typical of a newspaper's style. Because there is a very limited amount of space in a newspaper, journalists seek to present lots of information as simply as possible.
The title is also typical of newspaper style in that it is very punchy. These are known as "headlines" and appear at the beginning of all newspaper articles. This headline is also a rhetorical question: we are invited to decide ourselves whether we are to read of heroic explorers, or simply "boys messing about". The next sentence subtly tells us what the journalist may actually believe: whatever we think of explorers, they still cost the taxpayer a lot of money to rescue them. The second half leaves out the usual article "the": "Either way, taxpayer gets rescue bill". This is again common in newspapers to save space, but it also makes it seem more urgent.

We then have a second, subsidiary headline: "Helicopter duo plucked from liferaft after Antarctic crash". It gives us the number of people, what has happened, and where it took place. It is a very concise piece of writing.

In this piece, the journalist uses many subtle techniques to hint at his point of view. While journalists try to aim to be as objective or impartial as possible, they can use irony or occasional metaphors to let us know what they really think. In this extract, we should look out for ways in which Morris is critical of the explorers, and of their lack of planning and realism in particular. The first paragraph (lines 1-3) starts by withholding information about the men, which serves to increase our curiosity about who has crashed in the Antarctic. It starts with a possessive pronoun: "Their last expedition ended in farce", but we don't know whose expedition it is yet. "Farce" means a foolish, unrealistic comic play. It is clear from this theatrical metaphor that the journalist Steven Morris has already made his mind up that these explorers are not to be taken seriously. Their last expedition ended when the Russians threatened a military interception when the unnamed explorers tried to cross the Bering Strait from the US to Russia. (The Bering Strait is a narrow stretch of water near the North Pole.)

The next paragraph gives us some more concrete details about the men, and when the incident took place. It happened "yesterday", and concerned British explorers Steve Brooks and Quentin Smith, which almost led to "tragedy" when their helicopter "plunged" into the sea off Antarctica. Morris cleverly uses the word "tragedy" – another metaphor of the theatre, this time a serious play – to contrast with the "farce" or comedy of their last, failed expedition to Russia. Morris uses very strong, active verbs in describing what has happened to the explorers. The helicopter "plunged" (line 5) into the ocean, and the men "were plucked" from the icy water by a Chilean ship (line 7). The word "plunged" means to fall quickly into water her, and "plucked" means to be pulled quickly out of danger. The resemblance of the two verbs, and the repeated "pl" sounds, increases the sense of violent impact and daring rescue. There is also a sense of onomatopoeia here – the "pl" sounds recalls falling into water, which is why it is used in the common word "plop". The rescue took nine hours, and only took place after Mr Brooks' wife Jo Vestey was contacted by satellite phone, and she in turn made contact with the Royal Nay, RAF and British Coastguards.

The next paragraph (lines 10-11) hints that the men's adventure and rescue had attracted some criticism. There was resentment "in some quarters" that it had cost Chile and the UK a lot of money. The journalist here is using this vague phrase so they do not have to name their sources. The next paragraph (line 12) opens with a similarly vague statement – unnamed "experts" have questioned the wisdom of taking such a small helicopter (named as the single-engined Robinson R44) into the "hostile environment" of the Antarctic. The word "hostile" here is often used of people, and the Antarctic area is being personified as dangerous. The journalist then refers to a website promoting the Bering Strait expedition to try to clear up confusion about what the men were planning to do. Brooks and Smith claimed to be planning to fly from the North to South Pole in what their own website calls their "trusty helicopter". This phrase is in quotation marks in the article, because the author is trying to draw attention to the irony of this statement. It is certainly not trusty because we know it is a small helicopter – and it has clearly crashed.
We learn that Mr Brooks' wife had no idea "what the pair were up to". This is a very colloquial piece of English, and verges on the humorous. The increasingly humorous tone of the article continues with the quotation from Ms Vestey which echoes the title of the piece. Mr Brook and Mr Smith are "boys messing about with a helicopter".

Lines 19-35 of the article consist of a separate narrative of the main events of the rescue as it unfolded. The author, though, still chooses words to emphasise his opinion that there is something potentially ludicrous about the adventure. Line 19 tells us that the "drama" began at 1am British Time; the word drama echoes the metaphors of "tragedy" and "farce" from earlier, and alerts us that the two men being rescued treated their adventure too lightly, and their trip as a mere game. We learn that Mr Smith is "also known as Q". While this is a short version of his real name Quentin, it is also an echo of the character "Q" from the James Bond films, who is an eccentric boffin who provides gadgets for Bond. Encounters between Bond and Q are always full of jokes. Again, this signals that Morris is finding the incident amusing, but also that Smith and Brooks are treating their adventure as being like a film narrative. However, we learn that at 1am the helicopter ditches into the sea and they are in genuine peril.

Mr Brooks calls his wife in London on a satellite phone (line 22) and we have a quote given from Ms Vestey that Brooks asks her whether she could "call the emergency people". This is amusing because Ms Vestey is repeating Mr Brooks' polite but inept call for help.

The real call for help, though, comes from the ditched helicopter and Mr Brooks' emergency watch, both of which beam emergency signals. The watch was a wedding present, we learn (line 25) so we cannot even give Mr Brooks the credit for being prepared, it seems the journalist is trying to imply. The coastguard at Falmouth in Cornwall deciphers or decodes the signals and the RAF pass these on to the Royal Navy, whose ice patrol ship HMS Endurance "begins steaming" 180 miles to the scene, dispatching its two Lynx helicopters. The metaphor "steaming" doesn't mean the ship is literally steam-powered – it simply means it is moving quickly. It also has connotations of older ships, which are steam-powered, and may imply that Brooks and Smith are behaving like explorers from an earlier more reckless age, rather than living in the modern world.

Morris here gives us significant amounts of detail, which gives a vivid sense of the urgency of the scene, as well as the size of the task. We also learn of the danger, as one of the two helicopters is "driven back" by poor visibility, and the second is on its way when the two adventurers are eventually picked up by a Chilean vessel at 10.20 am – the man having been in the raft for over nine hours.

The narrative concludes with a quote from an unnamed Antarctic explorer, who told Mr Brooks' wife that it was "nothing short of a miracle" that the men had survived. A miracle means something almost magical, that cannot be rationally explained; the use of this metaphor makes us aware just how unlikely the rescue is, and how the men are fortunate to escape with their lives.

The second half of the extract develops the context for the story. It tells us about the backgrounds of the two men. We learn that both men are "experienced adventurers" (line 36). This is informative writing, in that it seeks to give a lot of detail in a concise form. On the surface Mr Brooks seems to be well qualified for being an explorer. On top of being a qualified mechanic and pilot, he has been to 70 countries in 15 years, trekked solo to Everest, and "walked barefoot for three days" in the Himalayas. However, when we learn he has been over rapids and "survived a charge by a silver back gorilla", we might suspect that the journalist Steven Morris is being facetious, or not taking the men seriously. By piling up these details, he makes them seem ridiculous and overblown. There is more evidence that Morris is not impressed by these credentials when he describes how Mr Smith "claims to have been flying since the age of five" (line 43). The word "claims" introduces doubt about Mr Smith's truthfulness, and is an example of innuendo. However, Morris does not openly question that Mr Smith has twice flown a helicopter around the world, and won a world freestyle flying competition. Morris manages to imply cleverly that these claims count for nothing. The next paragraph is a very short sentence (lines 46-7) which introduces a description of their Bering Strait failure: "Despite their experience, it is not the first time they have hit the headlines for all the wrong reasons".

Lines 48-55 give us an account of the ill-fated Russian expedition. Morris establishes immediately when it happened, in April. Mr Brooks and another explorer, Graham Stratford, were "poised" to complete a crossing of the 56-mile wide Bering Strait between the US and Russia. The vehicle, Snowbird VI, which they were using was "amphibious", which means it can go on land and on water. Morris uses very few metaphors in this extract but he uses the verb "carve" which lets us know that boat can go through ice like a sharp knife. Morris starts the next paragraph with a conjunction, "But" (line 53) to describe how suddenly all these plans went wrong. The Russian authorities threatened to send military helicopters to lift them off the ice. The military term "scramble" is used, which means to take off in a hurry to engage the enemy.

Morris ends his description of this failure by hinting how comic the episode was. "Ironically", the expedition was meant to show "good relations" between east and west (lines 54-55). Morris now provides a quotation by an expert. This is often done in newspaper articles to reinforce the opinion of the journalist, or to provide extra information. The expert called in questions the "wisdom" of the expedition, and we are told (line 56) that this expert is only one of a number who feel the same way. The expert, Günter Endres, is the editor of "Jane's Helicopter Markets and Systems". This is a well-known and respected publication. The publishing house "Jane" also publishes the famous "Jane's Fighting Ships", which is the definitive guide to the world's naval forces. We are therefore encouraged to believe that Endres is an expert, and to trust his word over the opinion of Morris. Endres is very candid in his assessment. He is "surprised" they chose the helicopter they did, and he gives his own view: "I wouldn't use a helicopter like that". Brooks and Smith were pushing the range of the helicopter "to the maximum" (line 59).

As opposed to the Mr Endres with his excellent qualifications, Brooks and Smith in the next paragraph are represented by an anonymous spokesman, who tells the reader that no-one knows what has gone wrong and that conditions were "excellent". This contrast with Endres' firm and precise views creates the impression once more that the men were incompetent.
We then return in the next paragraph (lines 62-64) to the sub-heading of the article. The Ministry of Defence – the part of the UK government responsible for its armed forces – comment that the "taxpayer would pick up the bill" and their spokesperson says it will be "highly unlikely" that any money will be recovered. This means that the UK government would have to pay for the costs of the rescue.

The final paragraph opens by telling the reader that Brooks and Smith are on their way to Eduardo Frei, a Chilean base, where HMS Endurance would pick them up.
It is ironic that the ship that sent helicopters and would ultimately pick them up is called HMS Endurance. An earlier ship of the same name was used by the explorer Sir Ernest Shackleton in one of the most famous polar adventures of all time, the 1914 expedition to the South Pole. Although the expedition ended in failure with the loss of the ship, all men survived due to Shackleton's strength of will and leadership. Morris does not draw the comparison overtly, but the fact he mentions the ship three times in the paragraph would make the reader who is familiar with Shackleton's story aware of the allusion, to the detriment of Mr Brooks and Mr Smith.

The paragraph closes by giving the last word to Ms Vestey, Mr Brooks' wife. Morris refrains from comment, which means that there is no contradiction of Ms Vestey's comment that "they'll probably have their bottoms kicked and be sent home the long way". Vestey is describing Brooks and Smith as naughty boys who will be subject to corporal punishment – as if they were misbehaving children in a book from the early twentieth century, for example. This seems to underplay the very real danger they were in and the massive efforts required to rescue them, but at the same time it also diminishes the heroism of what they were trying to achieve. They were not brave explorers like Shackleton, but ill-prepared for the dangers of the Antarctic, Morris is implying.

Between a Rock and a Hard Place by Aron Rolston

Biography

Aron Rolston was born in the USA in 1975. After studying mechanical engineering at Carnegie Mellon University in Pittsburgh, he moved to Colorado to continue mountaineering, which had become his major interest. In 2003, the accident which changed his life took place – as outlined below. Since then, his best-selling book has been made into an Oscar-nominated film, "127 Hours", by Danny Boyle, and he has continued with mountain climbing and media appearances.

Background

In April 2003, while hiking in Canyonlands National Park in Utah, Ralston was trapped by a rockfall. After five days, on the point of death, he was able to free himself from a narrow canyon by amputating his right arm at the wrist using a small hunting knife. After stumbling upon a group of hikers, he was finally rescued.

Summary

The extract is a narration of a single, dramatic episode. Aron Ralston is hiking in a remote part of the United States, and moving through a narrow gulley. The passage gives detailed descriptions of the way that Ralston normally tackles such spaces, and his climbing technique for doing so, but as he hangs from a boulder temporarily, it shifts and begins to move. He falls and the boulder crushes and traps his hand against the side of the canyon. The extract describes very intensely his pain, and his emotions faced with this predicament. It ends with Ralston trying to free his hand by moving the boulder, but he is unable to do so.

Analysis

The title of the piece is a well-known saying. It means to be stuck between two equally bad options. However, it is usually used metaphorically. As we discover in this passage it is literally true for Ralston.

The passage is in the first person, which is usual for an autobiographical piece. It is also in the present tense, which is less usual. This means that events are unfolding in front of us. The narrative voice is unaware of what will happen in the future. It makes the story much more exciting for the reader. The first sentence (line 1) is short: "I come to another drop-off". A "drop-off" is a sudden drop in floor level in the canyon (or narrow valley) that he is exploring. The height of this drop-off is "maybe eleven or twelve feet". The use of the word "maybe" here alerts us to the fact that Ralston is in an unfamiliar location, and therefore potentially in far great risk. Ten minutes before Ralston had descended a lower drop-off. This new feature has a "refrigerator chock-stone". A chock-stone is a rock wedged between the two sides of the canyon, forming a small tunnel below.

The word "refrigerator" here is a metaphor; the stone is of the same size and shape as the kitchen appliance. This everyday word gives a sense of scale to the reader, who might be unfamiliar with the geography of such features.

The first sign that Ralston is potentially in peril comes in the use of the adjective "claustrophobic" to describe the small tunnel under the chock-stone (line 4). Claustrophobia is the fear of closed spaces. Sufferers may fear being trapped. The sense of a narrow, confined place is developed in the final few sentences of the opening paragraph. Instead of the canyon walls widening or the bottom of the canyon opening into a bowl, the "slot" of the canyon "narrows to a consistent three feet across at the lip of the drop-off". The thin canyon continues for another fifty feet.

The second paragraph of the extract (lines 8-14) is a digression, when Ralston takes us away from the events he is narrating. He is concerned here with explaining for the reader climbing techniques that he uses. He opens the paragraph with "sometimes" (line 8), which moves us into the past, although he uses the present tense throughout. In "narrow passages" like this one Ralston uses a technique in which he turns sideways to the direction of the canyon, and pushes in one direction with his back, and another direction with his feet. He can control what he calls "counterpressure" (line 10) by replacing the pressure of his feet with that of his hands, and by doing this Ralston can move "up or down the shoulder-width crevice fairly easily as long as the friction contact stays solid" between him and the wall. This is a length technical explanation. Ralston uses very precise language here, and seems to address the reader directly, using the second person of the verb. He explains why this technique is called stemming or "chimneying": "you can imagine using it to climb up the inside of a chimney" (lines 13-14).

The third paragraph (lines 15-19) takes us back into the narrative. Ralston again focuses upon describing the scene. In line 15 he uses a contraction, "I'm" instead of I am, in the narrative for the second time, after the use of "it's" in line 8. This creates a sense again that he is addressing us directly in everyday spoken language, bringing us vividly in his experience. Just below where Ralston is standing is a smaller chockstone the size of a "large bus tire". Again Ralston uses objects from our everyday lives so we can understand what he is seeing. Ralston considers using this as a stepping stone, which reduces the drop from twelve feet to nine feet, which would be smaller than the drop-off he has already navigate. He again gives us a description of what he is aiming to do. He moves to the future tense, as we see him planning his next move: "I'll dangle off the chockstone, then take a short fall onto the rounded rocks piled on the canyon floor" (lines 17-19). The words "rounded rocks" use alliteration here to focus the reader's attention onto them, just as Ralston himself is focussing his attention on landing on these rocks as his ultimate goal in descending into the relative safety of the bottom of the canyon.

The next paragraph opens with a present participle, "stemming" (line 20), which plunges the reader immediately into the action, as Ralston starts moving out across the canyon, "with one foot and one hand on each of the walls". He traverses or crosses out to the chockstone. Ralston describes very carefully the way that he positions his body across the narrow canyon. He turns 45 degrees and places his back against the south wall, locks out his left knee, which pushes his foot against the opposite wall. This allows Ralston to kick the chockstone which was as big as a tyre. Ralston then uses a short sentence, which expresses how confident he is feeling at that point: "It's jammed tightly enough to hold my weight" (lines 23-24). Ralston steps onto it. We get the first hint that something might not be right: "It supports me but teeters slightly". Ralston decides that he does not want to chimney down from the chockstone, so he squats, grips the rear of the boulder, turns and decides to slide down, and lower himself from his "fully extended arms". This is "akin to climbing down from the roof of a house" (line 28). Tension in the reader has been building up throughout this passage.

Ralston hangs from the stone at the start of the next paragraph. Things begin to go badly wrong. Ralston uses the technique of personification in writing about the stone, as if it has life: "I feel the stone respond to my adjusting grip with a scraping quake" (line 29). Ralston's body applies "enough torque to disturb it from his position". The word "torque" is a technical term which means rotational force. Ralston "instantly" knows there is a problem, and "instinctively" he lets go of the rock and falls back onto the floor of the canyon. The two adverbs look and sound similar; each reinforces the others meaning, which is that everything happens extremely quickly, and Ralston reacts speedily without thinking. Again Ralston uses personification: the boulder falling towards him "consumes the sky". This is a disturbing and unexpected metaphor. As the boulder gets nearer, it fills Ralston's field of vision and blocks out the sun, as if it were eating it like a monster. Ralston is now no longer in control of his own body: "Fear shoots my hands over my head". Ralston is trapped, and he cannot move backwards or he will fall. Ralston only has one option, to "push off the falling rock" and protect his head (line 34).

Dalston cleverly tries to slow down the sense of time in the next paragraph. He tells us that "The next three seconds play out at a tenth of their normal speed". Ralston makes the reader feel this slowing down of time through a subtle technique of pacing in the next sentence. He divides this second sentence in the paragraph into three parts, to mirror the fact he is talking about a three-second span of time: "Time dilates, as if I'm dreaming, and my reactions decelerate" (lines 35-36). The three parts of the sentences are different lengths: the second clause is longer than the first, and the third clause is longer than the second. There are three syllables in the first part ("time dilates"), then five syllables ("as if I'm dreaming") in the second, then nine syllables ("and my reactions decelerate") in the third. As each part gets longer, the words also get longer, and this symbolises time slowing down.

The alliteration of "d" sounds alerts us to the most important words: "dilates" or gets bigger, "dreaming", as if this is not real, and "decelerate", a long four-syllable word meaning to slow down. The reader has to slow down to read this long word. This is a very clever piece of writing indeed, and it prepares us for the start of the next sentence, a simple "In slow motion", followed by a colon, and a description of the impact in minute detail. We now understand that these very quick actions appear very slow to the terrified Ralston.

A series of very short clauses follow the colon. Each clause is separated from the other by a semi colon, as each clause represents one of the things that happens to Ralston as the rock falls and time goes so slowly. The verbs used in each clause are very violent. Firstly, the falling rock "smashes" Ralston's left hand against the south wall of the canyon. Instead of just saying he sees this, Ralston uses an odd phrase "my eyes register the collision" (line 37). Ralston appears a passive observer of what is going on – register means to notice and to understand, but it is a very emotionless and scientific verb. Ralston does manage to respond instinctively though. He is able to "yank" his left arm back as the "rock ricochets". The word "ricochets" means to bounce off, and is usually used to describe the sound of a bullet echoing from an obstacle. The "r" alliteration seems to mimic the sound. This seems to be an example of onomatopoeia – or when the sound of a word or phrase represents the meaning. The boulder then "crushes" Ralston's right hand and "ensnares" his arm at the wrist. The word "ensnares" is a metaphor of hunting – again Ralston uses personification to make the rock seem evil, as if it meant to hunt and trap him like a hunter would its prey. Again, another short clause filled with violent verbs appears, and the rock slides down the wall dragging Ralston's arm, "tearing" the skin off the lateral or far side of his forearm. Ralston says that the rock slid down with his "arm in tow". This metaphor is taken from shipping – when a ship tows another immobile boat or barge. This makes his arm almost into an inanimate object, and prepares us for the shock of the last two paragraphs which follow this one.

After these breathless descriptions of the terrible accident, Ralston finishes the paragraph with a very short fragment of a sentence: "Then silence" (line 41). The accident has finished, the rock has fallen, and Ralston is left alone.

Ralston cannot believe what has happened to him. He tells us (line 43) that this disbelief "paralyzes" him temporarily when confronted with the aftermath of the accident. He sees his arm "vanishing into an implausibly small gap between the fallen boulder and the canyon wall" (line 43). Increasingly Ralston starts using language which makes a distinction between his mind, and his body. This is because he is only in control of his mind, whereas his body is trapped, and he is unable to do anything about it. He is powerless to control his body's pain, for example, as his "nervous system's pain response overcomes the initial shock" (line 44). Ralston introduces a very short sentence: "Good God, my hand" which helps us imagine exactly what he is thinking at the time. The "flaring agony" makes him panic. The word "flaring" is often used to describe sudden pain, and is a metaphor from fire – like flame flares up when an item combusts. The next line "I grimace and growl" uses the "gr" alliteration, and the onomatopoeia of "growl", to bring to life both the sounds Ralston makes and the expressions he pulls as he is trapped. Again he imagines his mind trying to command his body, even giving the mind a separate voice: "Get your hand out of there!" but he cannot remove it, even after trying to "yank" it free in a "naïve" or childish attempt to free it. The final sentence of this paragraph (line 47) is very short: "But I'm stuck". Starting with a conjunction, it expresses Ralston's sudden understanding of the hopelessness of his situation.

The final paragraph is filled with literary techniques and vocabulary that try to express Ralton's desperation and his pain. It opens with a startling image "Anxiety has my brain tweaking". This odd word means to pinch, painfully, but it also has a more up-to-date meaning in America. The word "tweaking" can refer to the painful and disorientating symptoms of hard drug withdrawal. It is followed by "searing-hot pain shoots from my wrist up my arm". The vowel sound "ea" in searing echoes "tweaking", and the compound adjective of "searing-hot" echoes "flaring agony", again using a metaphor of fire and heat. Again, Ralston emphasises how his mind tries to find a way to control the situation and escape. He remembers a "probably apocryphal" or doubtful story about a mother who, filled with adrenaline or stress hormones after an accident, lifted a crashed car to free her child (line 50). The fact that Ralston uses the words "conjures up" in recalling this story means he knows that this is a slim chance, as this is a metaphor from magic, when a magician makes something appear from thin air. He seems to know his effort is not realistic, and that he will not rationally be able to summon up the strength.

However, Ralston may indeed know that his situation is desperate, but he has to try. He knows it is "even odds" the story is made up – this is a metaphor taken from gambling and means there is a 50:50 chance the story is false. He says that *right now* it is his best chance, emphasising the urgency by putting this phrase into italics. He uses more violent imagery, telling us that his "body's chemicals are raging at full flood", a metaphor made even more striking by the use of alliteration. This means he realises that his adrenaline is coursing through his body, and that he will never be as strong as he is at that moment. He realises that he has to use "brute force" to try and move the boulder from his hand. He shoves against the boulder and uses a series of present participles of verbs of physical effort: he is "heaving", "pushing" and "lifting" the boulder with his knees pressed under the rock itself. The reader can imagine the continuous effort Ralston is exerting. He gets "good leverage" due to a shelf in the rock. Again, he carries on his effort (lines 55-56), with more verbs of active physical effort, such as "thrust" and "brace", and we read he is doing this "repeatedly", while grunting out loud the words "Come on…move". But the final sentence of the extract is very upsetting, and composed of one word only: "Nothing". Ralston has tried his hardest, but the rock will not move at all.

Young and dyslexic? You've got it going on by Benjamin Zephaniah

Biography

Benjamin Zephaniah was born in Birmingham in 1958, to parents from Barbados and Jamaica. He left school at 13, unable to read and write, due to his dyslexia. After drifting into petty crime, he decided to move to London at the age of 22 and concentrate upon his poetry, after learning to read at adult education classes. He published his first collection of poems in 1980, and since then has released a number of poetry collections, recordings, and novels. He rejected the OBE due to his strong republican political opinions, and has campaigned for Amnesty International. He has received honorary degrees from a number of Universities (including Birmingham, Exeter, and the University of Central England), and recently has been seen on the BBC in the series "Peaky Blinders".

Background

This extract appeared in a book, "Creative, Successful, Dyslexic" (Jessica Kingsley, 2015), which is an anthology of accounts by a number of high-achieving people who have dyslexia, including Sir Richard Branson, Eddie Izzard and Darcey Bussell. Zephaniah's piece was reprinted in the online edition of *The Guardian*, which means that the author is trying to reach the widest possible audience.

Summary

Zephaniah addresses this piece of writing to those who have dyslexia. He tries to get fellow dyslexics to understand that they see the world in a different, more creative way. However, he does not hide the fact that it can be hard to be different. He illustrates this throughout the extract by telling a number of stories about his own childhood. Zephaniah was dismissed at school, both for his dyslexia, and because he was a young black man. He was sent to borstal, where he decided to confront the future that had been mapped out for him, and take control of his life. Zephaniah starts to write poetry, and he goes to adult education classes to learn to read and write. Zephaniah finally becomes a professor of poetry and creative writing. He finishes the extract by reminding readers that dyslexics should celebrate and be proud of their difference, which requires them to be more creative than most people.

Analysis

The title of this article includes a piece of American slang, "you've got it going on". This means that young dyslexic people are very fortunate. We should expect therefore that Zephaniah is trying to reverse any prejudice that someone with dyslexia is to be pitied and treated as somehow less than other people. Zephaniah is going to try throughout the extract to challenge and overturn our preconceptions.

The first paragraph picks up the challenge of this title, and tries to make the reader understand the positive angle of those who have dyslexia. Zephaniah, as throughout the extract, uses his own story and personal experience to challenge the reader's expectations, and illustrate the difficulty fellow dyslexics face. He tells us that he "suffered" as a child, but learned to turn his dyslexia to his advantage, "to see the world more creatively". It is this creativity he will turn to again and again throughout the extract. He finishes the short first paragraph with a finely balanced sentence: "We are the architects, we are the designers". He moves from the first person singular in "I suffered" to the first person plural in "we"; he is keen to stress that sufferers are not alone but are part of a wider, creative community (lines 1-2).

Zephaniah was born in Birmingham in 1958, and he stresses he grew up in a different period, being "of the generation where teachers didn't know what dyslexia was" (line 3). He uses repetition to emphasise the education system was inadequate. There was "no education, no understanding and no humanity". However, Zephaniah is keen to let us know his analysis is not simply motivated by bitterness: " I don't look back and feel angry with the teachers" (line 5). He understands that it was the system that was at fault. He notes that then "being kind" and "listening to problems" was not usual. He then makes a pun on "kind" by saying "the past is a different kind of country". This is a deliberate misquotation of a very famous opening line of a book, L P Hartley's *The Go-Between*, about a doomed love affair in England just before World War One, narrated by an old man, who as a young boy was central to the dramatic events. Hartley actually writes "The past is a foreign country: they do things differently there". By introducing the word "kind", he stresses that the past was an unkind place.

The next few paragraphs of the extract explain just how different, and just how unkind, the past was for Zephaniah. In line 9 Zephaniah tells us that his ideas always "contradicted" or disagreed with those of his teachers. He gives us an anecdote or personal story. Thinking very imaginatively, Zephaniah responds to one of his teachers who told the class that "human beings sleep for one-third of their life". Zephaniah responds that "if there's a God" that this is a "design fault" and that God should have "designed sleep so we could stay awake" and good people could "do one-third more good in the world".

It doesn't matter whether we agree with Zephaniah's point or not. Even he realises that when the teacher disagrees with it, and says that "Bad people would do one-third more bad", she has a point. What he is upset with is that he is immediately told to "Shut up, stupid boy" (line 14). The teacher has treated him with a lack of respect for his ideas, and labelled him as stupid just for thinking something different.

The next two paragraphs introduce another factor alongside dyslexia; it is the fact that Zephaniah is treated with disdain because he is black. Zephaniah recalls another incident, and again he uses reported speech. He remembers a teacher talking about Africa and using the phrase "local savages". This is a racist phrase that shows an ignorance about the peoples of Africa and their lives. When Zephaniah responds with "Who are you to talk about savages?" he is reprimanded with a dismissive phrase "How dare you challenge me?" (line 19). Zephaniah's opinion is to be discounted, even in the face of such unfortunate and tactless comments by teachers in the past.

In the next paragraph, Zephaniah recalls asking a teacher for help when he was finding writing difficult. He is dismissed, rather than helped, and again Zephaniah recreates what the teacher told him. Zephaniah is told that "we can't all be intelligent" and he should try to be a "good sportsperson" and he should "go outside and play some football". Back then, Zephaniah recalls he thought this was "great", but from his older viewpoint, he realises the teacher was "stereotyping" him. The word stereotyping means that the teacher was labelling him, based upon a prejudice. The prejudice here is that a young black man cannot be academically intelligent, but should rely on abilities in sport to succeed. This is a racist attitude that dismisses someone's potential in an area simply because of the colour of his skin; because there are many talented black sportsmen, the teacher reasons, Zephaniah must be one, rather than being gifted in any other way. Zephaniah's plea for academic help is ignored.

The next paragraph (lines 24-27) introduces for the first time what Zephaniah eventually becomes famous for: poetry. He talks about the poems as existing even before they were written down: "I had poems in my head even then, and when I was 10 or 11 my sister wrote some of them down for me". Zephaniah, at age 13, could only read "very basically". He could only read enough to see "how much the banknote was worth", and he could always "ask a mate". These are very limited horizons, and talking of banknotes makes us realise that Zephaniah at this time could have chosen a poor path in life, obsessed by money.

Indeed the next paragraph lets us know that Zephaniah's education was cut short. He was "thrown out" of a lot of schools and eventually at age 13 he found himself in Borstal. Here "thrown out" is a metaphor, as he was not literally physically ejected, but this expresses well how society sought to discard him. He admits that part of the reason he was expelled was "for being a rude boy and fighting". A rude boy, in Jamaican slang, is a young man in a gang or engaged in petty crime. However, part of the reason Zephaniah was expelled was for "arguing with teachers on an intellectual level" (line 29). Zephaniah is at pains to let us know his crimes were not that serious, and "he didn't stab anybody". He did however "take revenge" on a teacher, by stealing his card and driving it one day into a front garden. This is clearly an anti-social act. However Zephaniah challenges out morality here by telling us that the teacher told the class that the "the Nazis weren't that bad". Zephaniah uses understatement here in the short sentence: "He could say that in the classroom". Zephaniah is implying that the education system tolerates people who say such shocking things, but is only too willing to punish him for his misdemeanours.

In Borstal, which is a special residential school for young offenders, Zephaniah tries to learn through observation of people, rather than through writing or conventional teaching methods. He watches fellow inmates and tries to work out what sorts of behaviour he is going to avoid. He gives the example of trying to avoid sitting like someone who is always slouched over. He finishes the paragraph with an emphatic sentence, which reads like a proverb or saying: "Being observant helped me make the right choices".

Zephaniah returns to his current situation in the next paragraph, after these memories of his early life, and puts these experiences into the context of modern society. He draws the surprising parallel that both the prison population, and the profession of architect, contain a high percentage of people with dyslexia. Looking at these statistics, Zephaniah admits, "I should be in prison". As a black man from a broken family home, in trouble with the police, illiterate and dyslexic, the chances of a bad outcome were very high. However, Zephaniah was able to take his chances in life and through willpower and effort overcome the obstacles he faced. He introduces the final sentence of this paragraph (lines 40-41) with a conjunction, "but", which makes it clear he does not feel bound to his fate: "I think staying out of prison is about conquering your fears and finding your path in life". There are two metaphors here: the first of battle, about defeating fear, and the second about finding a path – namely finding a clear way through the potential pitfalls. Zephaniah is using the first metaphor – of conquering fear – to emphasise that it will be a battle to beat the low expectations of society.

The next paragraph continues firmly in the present day, with Zephaniah telling us that he goes into prison to talk to people who are "in intelligence and other qualities" the same as him. He starts a sentence with a conjunction "but" and tells us that the only difference is that he took his opportunities and "they missed theirs, didn't notice them, or didn't take them". The language used here is deliberately plain and precise, as Zephaniah is not trying to impress the reader with effects, but to make his important point very strongly and simply.

Zephaniah never thought he was "stupid" (line 45). His "self-belief" (line 47) means that he can stand up for himself. If confronted by someone without dyslexia who claims that "black people are savages", Zephaniah tells himself that "I'm not stupid – you're the one who's stupid". This is another example of Zephaniah using reported speech to make the passage seem more immediate and alive.

In line 48, Zephaniah introduces the fact that he is a published poet. For his first book, he didn't write his poems down, he told them to his girlfriend. The poetry proved to be very popular "especially within the black community". Zephaniah became famous as a "dub" poet, which means he used language and pronunciation which came from black British and Jamaican slang. No-one considers that he wrote "dyslexic poems" because Zephaniah "wrote phonetically", which means that he tried to write in a way that reflected the way that real people spoke in his community. He wrote "wid luv" rather than "with love".

The next paragraph again uses the technique of giving an episode or vignette from Zephaniah's past to make a point. Zephaniah uses reported speech to make it dramatic. At 21 Zephaniah went to an adult education class to "learn to read and write". The teacher tells him he's dyslexic. Instead of using "I said" Zephaniah uses the slang expression "I was like" and then uses speech marks to give us his reaction: "Do I need an operation?" Zephaniah is using humour here to write about a serious situation. When the teacher explains what has happened, Zephaniah suddenly realises what he has been suffering from: "Ah, I get it. I thought I was going crazy".

Zephaniah (line 55) gives us a brief account of his career after this: "I wrote more poetry, novels for teenagers, plays, other books and recorded music". This is an incredible achievement, but Zephaniah follows it up with another claim, of which he seems even more proud, and which seems to be a paradox: "I take poetry to people who do not read poetry". However Zephaniah still has difficulty with aspects of writing. He has to use visual techniques to help him remember what he meant. So when he is trying to use the word "knot" he draws a picture, and if he can't spell "question" he just uses a question mark.

Although he is successful, Zephaniah still has some anxiety about reading. When he comes across a book, initially he sees "the size of it" and this makes him have empathy with "a lot of young people who find reading tough" (line 61). Zephaniah, even after being given the post of Professor of Poetry and Creative Writing at Brunel University, is anxious that the students will be "officially" more educated than he is. Again, he uses the technique of using direct speech to make his point more dramatic. He tells his students that although they can succeed and get the right grade, if they "don't have passion, creativity, individuality, there's no point". These abstract nouns represent what Zephaniah feels are more important than simply getting good results.

Zephaniah has reached the point where people can "accommodate" or find ways of working around his dyslexia. Zephaniah can perform his poems because he does not have to be "word perfect", but he still can't read one of his novels in public. He has to get an actor to read the words for him otherwise the concentration of reading means that "the mood is lost". Zephaniah opens the next paragraph with an aphorism. An aphorism is a short sentence which presents a truth or opinion in a concise and striking way. Zephaniah writes "If someone can't understand dyslexia it's their problem". This is also a reversal of normal thinking – dyslexia becomes a problem for other people, not the person with it, who is usually treated as deficient. Zephaniah again uses the analogy of race, and comes up with a witty and striking passage. If someone treats him badly because he is black, he does not think "How can I become white". Zephaniah then makes the most provocative statement in the whole piece, when he addresses a potential dyslexic with the following: "In many ways being dyslexic is a natural way to be" (line 74).

Zephaniah is not just being challenging for the sake of it. He is prepared to back it up with an analysis of the way that western writing works: "What's unnatural is the way we read and write" (line 75). Zephaniah notes that for pictorial languages such as Chinese, the symbols used resemble things, as he puts it "you can see the word for a woman because the character looks like a woman. The word for a house looks like a house". In English, the sounds are represented by an alphabet, and there is no link at all between the shape of a word and what it is trying to express. There is a lot of sibilance in his final sentence, which reinforces the sense that Zephaniah is focussing the reader's attention on words and sounds: "It is a strange step to go from that to a squiggle that represents a sound".

The next paragraph sees Zephaniah addressing a possible dyslexic reader directly, using slang to make the point very directly: "So don't be heavy on yourself". Heavy here means don't be depressed, but it is also metaphorical, in that people with dyslexia may feel that they are under a burden, weighed down by society's expectations. Zephaniah then moves to address the parents of dyslexics, asking them to consider that it isn't a "defect" and that "you may have a genius on your hands". Throughout the paragraph Zephaniah uses the second person of the verb, with "you" repeated throughout. He tells us that dyslexics are forced to be creative, when the normal words that everyone else would chose don't come easily to them, and that they "have to think of a way to write round it" (line 83). Zephaniah comes up with the striking metaphor of a "creativity muscles" to illustrate how working on being creative makes you better at it. Just like an athlete can build up their muscles through working out, we can make ourselves more creative through practice; this means that people with dyslexia are in control, not victims of dyslexia.

The final paragraph again uses Zephaniah's favourite technique in this extract, which is to dramatize his point with direct speech. He tells us that children say to him "I'm dyslexic too" and he tells them to use their difference to their advantage. He repeats the title of the piece, and echoes his opening paragraph "Us dyslexic people, we've got it going on – we are the architects. We are the designers". Because Zephaniah has been such a success, he becomes a role model for the children, and they are "proud" of his success. He had no such role models as a child. Zephaniah finishes the extract with an amusing sentence, ironically turning on its head the prejudice that "normal" people have: "Bloody non dyslexics … who do they think they are?" (line 88).

A Game of Polo with a Headless Goat by Emma Levine

Biography

Emma Levine is a British writer and photographer. Since graduating from University in 1992, she has travelled widely in Asia, reporting on local customs and sports in particular. She has written a number of books, and presented TV documentaries.

Background

For the travels collected in "A Game of Polo with a Headless Goat", Levine spent 13 months travelling through Asia, observing such odd sports as oil wrestling, donkey racing, and "horseback javelin".

Summary

In this humorous extract Levine is in Karachi, Pakistan, being driven by two young men to watch a donkey race. It opens with Levin waiting in their car at the top of a hill for the race to arrive, which takes a very long time, and she thinks that nothing will ever happen. Suddenly the donkeys appear, surrounded by scores of vehicles, and Levine and her companions drive out to join the throng following the race. Levine describes the danger and the thrill of the race, with lengthy passages filled with noise and colour. However, one of the donkeys falls, and Levine finds herself in the middle of a heated argument over the race, and remains in the car for her own safety, until the young boys arrive back and they drive off; Levine finally learns that her driver is underage.

Analysis

The extract is in the first person throughout, and in the past tense; these are typical choices for an autobiographical narrative, which is concerned with depicting incidents at a particular place and time.

It opens in the middle of the action, and we note that Levine is not alone. She uses the first person plural pronoun "we" to open the paragraph. She and her unnamed companions are in the car, trying "to find the best viewing spot", which is the "crest of the hill", allowing sight of the approaching race. Levine asks "the lads" if she can join in the "Wacky Races", which she puts into quotation marks (line 2). "Wacky Races" is an American cartoon TV series from the 1960s, in which a variety of participants travel across world in outlandish cars and vehicles. This allusion signals to the reader that we are to expect something extraordinary. The use of the phrases "the lads" tells us that Levine's companions are young men, but also it is a familiar term, which means she has some affection perhaps for them. Indeed, the lads are very enthusiastic about joining the race and following the donkeys.

Levine gives us their reaction in reported speech, which increases the immediacy of the scene; their plan is to stash Levine in the car boot, from which she can film the race, and they tell her their plan: "As the donkeys overtake us, we'll join the cars". Levine's question to the boys is ambivalent: "But will you try to get to the front?" It is impossible to be sure if she wants to get to the front, or whether she is timid or apprehensive about this. The response is very confident: "Oh yes, that's no problem". However the reader might see this as ironic, because in a narrative like this, it is likely that there is some danger involved.

The next paragraph contains a number of metaphors as Levine tries to convey the mixture of boredom and excitement that is involved in waiting for the donkey race to arrive. The two "lads", even though they have not usually been interested in the "Karachi sport" of donkey-racing are now "fired up with enthusiasm" (line 7). The metaphor "fired up" is taken from steam engines, and means that a strong fire has been set in the boiler; it suggests that Levine's companions are filled with enthusiasm and ready for action.

Levine then uses hyperbole or overstatement to express her growing anticipation, when she says they waited "for eternity". This means for all time, but is not to be taken literally, as it only an hour; it expresses humorously Levine's boredom. Like a bird, Levine is "perched in the boot", another striking metaphor. This means that she is not firmly in the car, but in a dangerous position, which increases the reader's anxiety that something dangerous and exciting is about to happen. However, she finishes this paragraph on a comic note, as an hour later she is passed by a "villager on a wobbly bicycle" who nearly falls off as he passes and gazes at Levine, peeping out of the boot with a "zoom lens pointing out". She had come to look at a strange spectacle, but ironically she has become a figure of strange amusement to the local population.
Levine builds up the tension further in the next paragraph. Donkey-carts pass, carrying spectators, and Levine and her companions call out to them. The only reply is "coming, coming". Levine herself starts to doubt she will see anything: "I was beginning to lose faith in its happening, but the lads remained confident" (line 12-13).

In the next paragraph, the race finally appears, just as Levin was assuming it had been cancelled. Levin concentrates on using metaphors of noise. The donkey-carts appear in a "cloud of fumes and dust" thrown up by fifty vehicles "roaring up in their wake". The word "wake" here is an image taken from sailing, and is the trail of disturbed water left behind after the passage of a ship or boat. Yaqoob, one of the boys accompanying Levine, "revved the engine". "Rev" is a word which is partly onomatopoeic, sounding like the noise of the car, but also an abbreviation of the word "revolution" meaning the engine turning over.

Levine then gives us a series of images to describe the physical appearance of the donkeys. They are "dwarfed" by the surrounding cars, but in spite of their size they are going at close to 40 kph. Levine uses a metaphor taken from horse-racing, describing the donkeys as "neck-and-neck", which means they are close together, with each donkey alternately getting its neck ahead. The jockeys are "perched" on top (lines 19-20), which echoes the way that Levine herself was "perched" in the boot of the car (line 7) waiting for the race, and has the same meaning – that the jockeys are in a dangerous position.

The jockeys are using whips "energetically, although not cruelly". The reader might think that Levine is romanticising the treatment of the donkeys here; it is hard to imagine that the use of the whips is not cruel. Levine could be criticised for getting carried away by the excitement and not thinking about the animals' welfare.

In the next paragraph Levine again focuses upon the sound, what she calls the "noise of the approaching vehicles". She uses onomatopoeia again, with a description of "horns tooting", which she follows up with another present participle in "bells ringing". Levine also breaks the narrative of the race in the passage to explain how the "special rattles" the crowd uses are made (they are a "metal container filled with fried beans", which work like the Mexican instrument, maracas). Levine finishes with a sentence filled with energy, and adds verbs of physical description and motion to her portrayal of the noise of the chase. Men are "standing" on top of their cars, "hanging" out of taxis or "perched" on lorries, and Levine users personification when she says that the vehicles "jostled" to get to the front of the convoy; this is a word that would normally be used for people moving together in a crowd. Again, she repeats the word "perched" continuing the theme of danger.

In the next paragraph (line 26) Levine introduces one of her drivers for the first time in this extract as "Yaqoob", and she continues with her strong use of visual imagery, and use of active verbs of motion. Yaqoob chooses the right time to "edge out" and "swerve" in front of the closest car, to give the "perfect place" to see the race. Levine tries two metaphors to express just how dangerous and lawless the whole enterprise is. It is "Formula One without rules", or a "city-centre rush hour gone anarchic". Formula One is the fastest and most dangerous form of motorsport, and without rules it would be deadly. Rush hour is the time when most cards are on the road. The word anarchic means without any laws. Both of these suggest that the race is out of control

Levine uses alliteration to emphasise this chaos, the hard "c" of "complete flouting" echoed in the words "common sense" and the last consonant of "anarchic".
The next paragraph focuses upon the race, and in particular Yaqoob's driving. Levin uses a metaphor usually associated with food (line 30) when she says that Yaqoob "relished" the race. To relish something means to enjoy it very much. This suggests that, in spite of the danger, Yaqoob is finding the whole event fun, in spite of the danger.
Levine then uses a scientific term, "the survival of the fittest". This is usually used in relation to the theory of evolution, and means that only the most suited or well-adapted creatures will thrive, and the less-adapted will die out. The metaphor here implies that only the best drivers will survive the race. Used in this context, the juxtaposition of the normally precise scientific language and the wild race is humorous. Yaqoob's driving would certainly not be suited to everyday traffic. Levine takes delight in listing these skills: the ability to "cut in front of a vehicle" (line 31); "nerves of steel"; "no lane discipline"; "an effective horn". There are "two races", the donkeys themselves and the following cars, and oncoming traffic has to take evasive action. Levine introduces as contrast to this rush of images a short sentence: "Yaqoob loved it". Yaqoob is in his element with "his language growing more colourful". This is a use of euphemism, or not speaking about something directly, and it means that Yaqoob is swearing and using bad language.

In Levine's next paragraph, the race is reaching its climax. The second sentence starts with the word "but" which is very ominous, and indeed there is a crash, ironically at the "hospital gate", the finishing line, when the leading donkey falls. Levine uses the word "swerve" again here, as she had done in line 23. Levin emphasises the sudden end of the race in the very short sentence that concludes the paragraph, "The race was over", repeating "over" to express its finality.

The next paragraph also opens with a very short sentence: "and then the trouble began" (line 43). This has a humorous effect, because the race has been so chaotic, it is hard to imagine even more trouble coming along. The race result is contested – it is not automatically, as Levine assumes, the donkey that remained on its feet. There were over a hundred "punters", or people who had placed bets on the race. To create a sense of the numbers of people disputing the result, Levin cleverly repeats the word "everyone" (lines 44 and 53). A sense of the growing sense of argument is created by the three part sentence that Levin uses to build the tension: "Voices were raised, fists were out and tempers rising".

The next paragraph introduces the name of the second young man with whom Levine was travelling in the race. His name was Iqbal. Both Yaqoob and Iqbal recognise the danger of the growing disturbance; the "v" sound repeated in "nervous" and "volatile" puts a stress on both words, and shows how they are getting more anxious. The word "volatile" means likely to explode or have a violent reaction, and is a metaphor taken from chemistry. Other sinister words are used by Levine. When she is left by the two young men, who have gone to see what is happening, she thinks that they are "swallowed up" by the crowd. Levine then switches to direct speech, to make what is happening more immediate and dramatic: "it's starting to get nasty. I think we should leave". As they drive away, Levine relieves the tension, again with a piece of direct speech. Yaqoob drives away slowly and then reveals the truth about this driving skills: "I don't even have my licence yet because I'm underage!"
Levine notes in the final paragraph that both of the young men found this to be "hilarious", but she reflects upon the consequence of what might have happened. The young and inexperienced driver could have caused a "massive pile-up" in the middle of the race. Levine finishes with a technique called litotes or understatement. He says that the pile up "could have caused problems". She doesn't have to spell out in great details what these problems could have been – serious injury, or perhaps even worse.

Beyond the Sky and the Earth: A Journey into Bhutan by Jamie Zeppa

Biography

Jamie Zeppa was born in 1964 in Ontario, Canada. After studying for an MA at York University, she spent two years teaching in Bhutan, the experiences leading to a successful book on her trip. She returned from Bhutan with her daughter from her failed marriage to a Bhutanese local, she wrote another book, a novel, and now lives in Toronto teaching English.

Background

When she was 24, Jamie Zeppa left Canada and abandoned her planned doctoral studies to teach English in Bhutan. The title of the memoir "Beyond the Sky and the Earth" is taken from a traditional expression in Bhutan, which expresses the depth of one's gratitude. The memoir covers her time teaching at Sherubtse College, and describes falling in love with her future husband, as well as humorous experiences she has with her fellow western teachers.

Summary

This extract describes the first experiences that Jamie Zeppa has arriving in Bhutan, an isolated country high in the Himalayas. It alternates between descriptions of what she sees and passages which explain the history and culture of the country. It opens with a lengthy, poetic description of the country from the air, as Zeppa flies in. Zeppa then describes two fellow Canadians who have come to teach in Bhutan as well. She then describes the town of Thimphu, and its history. Zeppa then goes on to describe the appearance and history of the native peoples of Bhutan, and concludes with a number of paragraphs that describe Bhutan's past, and the way it resisted occupation by colonial powers.

Analysis

This extract from the book is a memoir of a personal trip. As such, it is written primarily in the first person, and concentrates upon personal impressions of a place; however, throughout the extract there are longer passages of history or geography, which try to explain the history of the country she is visiting. Bhutan is an isolated, mountainous country in Asia, in the Himalayan plateau.

The opening paragraph starts with a fragment of a sentence – it has no main verb. The only verbs are present participles, "climbing" and "rolling" and describe the way in which the earth seems to be alive, and the mountain chain never-ending. Verbs in the present participle form are neither past nor future; there seems no way out of the mountains, they are all that the narrator can imagine. They are "all around", and form peaks and valleys "again and again" (line 1). The next sentence picks up this theme, of the timeless and all-encompassing nature of the mountains: "Bhutan is all and only mountains" (lines 1-2).

The next sentence is in the first person, as Zeppa establishes that this is going to be a narrative focused on her experiences. She is humble in the face of the mountains, and tells us that the scale of what she sees is beyond her comprehension. She knows "the technical explanation for the landscape", which is the collision of the Indian tectonic plate with the Asian land mass, but as she admits "I cannot imagine it" (line 4). Zeppa has to search for a more easily comprehensible metaphor. She imagines a "giant child" making the landscape. Again, Zeppa uses participle forms of the verb, ending in "ing" every time, and chooses very active, physical images: "gathering earth", "piling up rock", "pinching mud", "knuckling out little valleys and gorges", "poking holes". In this metaphor, the landscape is described as being made by a baby playing in the earth, using its knuckles and hands to shape the mountains. But it is a giant baby, which is impossible in reality. This is therefore a very startling set of images. We get the impression Zeppa is struggling to make sense of the vastness of the landscape in front of her, and the effect of Zeppa moving from the very small to the very large is to make the reader share in her wonder and confusion.

Zeppa then locates where she is, using the present tense in order to make her narrative immediate. She is in Thimphu, the Bhutanese capital city. The distances she has travelled to get there are enormous. The capital is a ninety-minute drive away from Paro airport – and it took "five different flights over four days" to fly from Toronto to Paro via Montreal, Amsterdam, New Delhi and Calcutta. In the modern world, this is a very long journey. Zeppa uses a short sentence to contrast with the length of her journey: "I am exhausted, but I cannot sleep" (line 9). Zeppa lets her imagination wander. She uses alliteration in the next sentence, to contrast her surroundings, a simple "pine-paneled room" in the hotel, with the view from the window: "I watch mountains rise to meet the moon". The juxtaposition of the room and the moon is made more striking because of the assonance or half-rhyme. The mountains are also personified; like a person they "rise to meet" the moon. This creates a dream-like, unreal quality. Zeppa shifts tenses into the past, telling us how she "used to wonder" what lay behind mountains. Now she knows, and she echoes the opening lines of the extract: "on the other side of mountains are mountains, more mountains and more mountains again" (lines 14-15). Her mind cannot comprehend the enormity of the Himalayan range.

Zeppa uses surprising compound adjectives. These are when two words are joined together to form a new one, and they are a powerful means of describing something. The plains of India are "baked-brown" (line 13). This shows both their appearance, but also hints at how hot they are. When she talks about the mountain she uses the words "wind-sharpened pinnacles", which describes how the knife-like ridges were created by the action of the wind. Again, the whole landscape is personified, with the earth described as a "convulsion of crests and gorges". Convulsion is a very violent word, and has a medical meaning, as when someone is suffering from a violent reaction or fit. This metaphor suggests that the landscape is very extreme, with the valleys very deep and the peaks very sharp. It also implies that the landscape is frightening to Zeppa as she encounters it for the first time.

After these vivid images, Zeppa finishes the paragraph with a different tone, as she gives us important geographical information which can help us visualise where she is. Just past Mount Everest, the world's highest peak, the Tibetan plateau is "the edge of a frozen desert 4,500 meters above sea level". We learn that Thimphu is at half that height, but "the winter air is thin and dry and very cold" (line 18).

Zeppa devotes her next paragraph to a description of her first morning in Bhutan. Breakfast is not very pleasant, and Zeppa uses a number of very negative adjectives to describe her breakfast. Again, she uses the present tense to make the scene more immediate, and show us she is experiencing something for the very first time. There is only "instant coffee" and "powdered milk", the white bread is "plasticky" and the "red jam" flavourless – she cannot even tell what fruit it once was. From this we can tell she is from a privileged western background, and that she is not comfortable with the potential deprivations of Bhutan. She meets two other Canadians who have signed on to teach in Bhutan for two years, Lorna and Sasha. Zeppa devotes most the description to Lorna. We are given extensive details on Lorna's hair (golden brown), her freckles, and her "home-on-the-farm demeanor", another interesting compound adjective. Zeppa means someone down to earth and practical, like a farmer. However, Lorna has a mischievous side shown in her "ringing laughter" and tales of "wild characters" from her home life in Saskatchewan. Sasha is merely described as "slight and dark, with an impish smile" (line 24). After meeting with Gordon, the director of the teaching programme, all three young women walk through Thimphu. Lorna and Sasha are more experienced, having travelled and worked abroad. Zeppa cleverly hints that she is overwhelmed and not completely happy about her arrival in Bhutan. Lorna and Sasha are "ecstatic" or delighted by Bhutan so far, but Zeppa admits otherwise: "I stay close to them, hoping to pick up some of their enthusiasm".

Zeppa continues to mix information about Bhutan with her own first impressions of the place. Thimphu appears to her smaller than its official 20,000 population. Zeppa notes that "it doesn't even have traffic lights", which is an odd observation, and shows that Zeppa was not prepared for how different this place appears from her limited experience. She is experiencing what can be termed "culture shock" – a sudden sense of being overwhelmed by how different something is. She expresses this by using vocabulary which appears vague, and stresses what she doesn't understand. Policemen directing traffic use "incomprehensible but graceful hand gestures". Buildings all look the same, they "all have the same pitched roof, trefoil windows and heavy beans painted with lotus flowers, jewels and clouds" (lines33-34). The small shops "seem to be selling the same things", which she lists. The objects on sale seem to disappoint her, and she uses very negative imagery to describe the "packages of stale, soft cookies from India – Bourbon Biscuits, Coconut Crunchies and the hideously colored Orange Cream Biscuits". She sees more evidence of the west than she thought: "There are more signs of the outside world than I had expected", and these include a very odd range of things, such as Willie Nelson's music, a Rambo poster, and "teenagers in acid washed jeans".

She calls these "cultural infiltration", which is a very negative metaphor which expresses her opinion about western influence, being an image which suggests both spying and contamination. To infiltrate, in the world of espionage, means to enter secretly, often with the purpose of causing harm. This implies that the western world is very negative and threatening. She seems to have a stereotype before arriving that the country would have no modern influence whatsoever, and seems disappointed it does. Nevertheless, she sees these signs of the modern world as rare and "startling against the Bhutanese-ness of everything else". The word "Bhutanese-ness" is a neologism or new word, made up by Zeppa to describe something for which she cannot find the vocabulary – it means something essentially from Bhutan.

We gain a different perspective on the town in the next paragraph, as Gordon's voice is introduced. Although the town seems very old, with "cracked sidewalks and faded paintwork", it is only thirty years old at the most. It was built by the third king as a new capital, around a small village and a *dzong* or fortress. The paragraph ends both amusingly, and ominously, when Gordon tells Zeppa that Thimphu will "look like New York" after a year in the east. The implication is that the rest of Bhutan is even less developed (lines 47-48).

Zeppa gives a further description of the town in the next paragraph, focussing on the "Taschichho Dzong" or seat of the Royal Government of Bhutan. We get a hint that this place is an absolute monarchy, not a republic or constitutional monarchy that exists in the west. Zeppa uses more compound adjectives to describe the "red-roofed, golden-tipped" fortress, but apart from this large building, the countryside gets more deserted, and wilder. The terraced fields are "barren" and "merge into forest". Zeppa does not believe Gordon: "Thimphu will never look like New York to me, I think" (lines 53-54).

Zeppa devotes the next paragraph to describing the Bhutanese people. She calls them a "very handsome people" and quotes a traveller from 1774, George Bogle, who calls them the "best built race of men I ever saw". The adjectives Zeppa uses are extremely positive. Zeppa says that the locals have "beautiful aristocratic faces with dark, almond-shaped eyes, high cheekbones and gentle smiles". She is trying to make us see the Buthanese with fresh eyes, free of prejudice.

Zeppa continues to describe the traditional dress of the men and women. The women wear a "kira" or ankle dress and the men a "gho", a form of large kimono. We should not forget the jeans, though, worn by the young people. Zeppa also tells us that Bhutanese of Nepali origin are taller and darker. Zeppa and the other foreigners there do not attract significant attention, and Gordon had mentioned the "small but friendly 'ex-pat' community". The word "ex-pat" means foreigner, often used of westerners in another country.

Zeppa continues to be impressed by the Bhutanese, and also continues to be unable to find the right words to express just what she finds so impressive. The young man behind the counter of a hotel speaks "impeccable" or perfect English to her, and this causes her to "search" for the right word to describe the people. No "single word" can capture the quality of "dignity, unselfconsciousness, good humor, grace" that she finds in the people (lines 67-69).

In the final two paragraphs of the extract, Zeppa moves away from her own immediate, personal experiences to give the reader a history of Bhutan. She moves to the past tense: "In Thimphu, we attended a week-long orientation session" with other English-speaking volunteers from around the world. Zeppa found the lessons on Bhutanese history the most interesting, and she gives a summary or précis of the last 1,000 years of the area. The country was settled by Tibetan immigrants around the tenth century CE, but had been inhabited before that. Buddhism had arrived around the eight century CE, and it absorbed the local religion, Bon. The region was only unified under one authority in the seventeenth century by the Tibetan Lama Ngawang Namgyel, under the name of Druk Yul, the "Land of the Thunder Dragon". Zeppa avoids her writing being a simple dry list of historical events by focussing on the beauty and poetry of the names of the country. These includes "the Southern Land of Medicinal Herbs" and "Sandalwood Country". District names also interest Zeppa. She uses the compound adjective "felicitously-named", which means that these names have the good fortune also to be beautiful. They include the "Lotus Grove of the Goods", the "Rainbow District of Desires" and the "Land of Longing and Silver Pines". However, we don't know what these sounded like in the local languages, so they might be less beautiful than in English. The word "Bhutan" has a more ordinary origin, it comes from "Bhotanta" or the "end of Tibet", from the Sanskrit "Bhu-uttan" or highlands. Sanskrit is the original ancient language of India, and is related to English and most other European languages.

Zeppa's final paragraph gives the history of the rare western visitors to Bhutan. She makes a pun on the phrase "hue and cry" which means a commotion. She says Asia was being "overrun" by European visitors of "varying hue but similar cry". This means Europeans of different nationality but the same aim – to colonise and dominate. Only Portuguese Jesuits (a type of Roman Catholic priest) came in the seventeenth century, and asix "brief" British missions came from the 1700s onwards. However relations with the British took "a nasty turn" when Ashley Eden visited in 1864. Zeppa uses humour and bathos to describe Eden's treatment as he sought to stop Bhutanese raids on British territory. Eden "had his back slapped, his hair pulled, and his face rubbed with wet dough" (lines 92-93) before signing a treaty that led to a brief war between the British and Bhutanese. Zeppa is filled with admiration for the way that the Bhutanese resisted the "British empire in the south, and the Great Game being played out in the north between the colonial powers". The "Great Game" is a metaphor which is used to refer to the way that the great powers such as Great Britain and Russia fought for dominance in Asia in the nineteenth century as the Ottoman Empire (modern day Turkey) collapsed and lost its territories. The word "game" is used ironically, because it was not a game, but led to serious conflict, such as the Crimean War. Zeppa admires the spirit of the Bhutanese for not being taken over as part of this conflict.

H is for Hawk by Helen Macdonald

Biography

Helen Macdonald was born in England in 1970. She studied English Literature at Jesus College, Cambridge. After working in falcon conservation she was a Research Fellow at Jesus College between 2004 and 2007. She has written extensively on the natural world, and in 2014 her memoir "H is for Hawk" won the Samuel Johnson prize for non-fiction.

Background

"H is for Hawk" tells the story of Helen Macdonald's attempt to cope with her violent grief, after the sudden death of her father. She finds herself single, nearly middle-aged, and about to finish her job as an academic at a Cambridge college, and in search of a permanent place to live. To try and find some meaning in her increasingly chaotic life, she decides to train a young goshawk, a beautiful but difficult bird of prey to handle. Her father had introduced her to the world of falconry, and she believes it will honour his memory. In between the story of her training of the hawk, Macdonald describes the experience of a much earlier writer, T H White, who in "The Goshawk" (1951) wrote of his struggles to tame the bird.

Summary

In this extract, Macdonald has travelled to pick up a young goshawk from a breeder. Macdonald describes using very poetic language the intense experience of opening the box to see the bird for the first time. She also imagines what it must feel like for the young bird to see the wider outside world for the first time. However, she discovers that, due to a mix-up, the breeder has shown her the wrong bird. She does not like the other, larger, bird and pleads with the breeder to let her keep the first bird she saw.

Analysis

The extract opens right in the middle of the encounter between Macdonald and the man who is selling her the goshawk. Macdonald makes it immediate by using direct speech, as if we are there. The man says he needs to "check the ring numbers against the Article 10s", which are the yellow forms he pulls out. These forms introduce a key theme: the tension between freedom and captivity. Because the bird is a "captive-bred rare bird" it must have all the correct paperwork throughout its life. Also, the man is keen that Macdonald does not get the wrong bird. The first paragraph is deliberately restrained and low-key, which will form a contrast with the extremely poetic and startling language in the paragraphs to follow.

The next paragraph, though, continues to build the tension quietly. It opens with a short, bald sentence: "We noted the numbers". Macdonald and the man don't act, they just look at the boxes containing the birds, and she stresses how flimsy and ordinary the containers look: "We stared at the boxes, at their parcel-tape handles, their doors of thin plywood and hinges of carefully-tied string" (lines 5-6). Then, the man acts, but very slowly, untying a hinge and squinting into the "dark interior". As in a horror film, there is a sudden, startling sound, which after the quiet has a powerful effect: "A sudden *thump* of feathered shoulders and the box shook as if someone had punched in, hard, from within" (lines 7-8). The word *thump* in italics gives it added emphasis. The man's reaction is ominous, and he frowns when he tells Macdonald the bird has her hood off. The hood, as Macdonald explains, was "to keep the hawk from fearful sights". She then finished the paragraph with a very startling two-word sentence: "Like us". She cleverly reverses the usual idea that we should be scared of wild predators. We are the fearful sights.

The next paragraph, lines 11-31, contains a lot of literary devices, and a lot of very dramatic and unexpected imagery. The first ten sentences only contain one main verb. They are very short and fragmentary, and serve to slow down the sense of time, creating tension. The first three emphasise a pause: "Another hinge untied. Concentration. Infinite caution." The repeated hard "c" and "t", and the "n" sounds set up a slow rhythm like the ticking of a clock. The next image is startling, with "Daylight irrigating the box." Irrigation is not used with the sun, usually, but with water, and it means to bring water to a dry area; this unexpected mixing up of images has two effects. Firstly, it makes us focus more closely on the experience of Macdonald and the hawk; secondly, it prepares us for a paragraph in which Macdonald will be using very unfamiliar language to make us see the world in new ways, as the goshawk experiences the world for the very first time.

The sentences remain short, but sound is introduced: "Scratching talons, another thump. And another. *Thump.*" Again, Macdonald uses another strange image, the air turning "syrupy, slow, flecked with dust." Ominously, she says that it is the "last few seconds before a battle" (line 13). After all of these short sentences and clauses, a long sentence from lines 13-17 finally uncoils, as the goshawk leaves the box. This sentence is so complicated, and there are so many different techniques that we need to slow down here and break it into different parts.

The sentence starts in the simple past tense, but opens with the word "And", keeping up the momentum: "And with the last bow pulled free, he reached inside". The tense then changes suddenly to the present tense, and the writing becomes deliberately confusing, to mimic Macdonald's shock, and the shock of the hawk as it is released into the daylight: "amidst a whirring, chaotic clatter of wings and feet and talons and a high-pitched twittering and it's all happening at once, the man pulls an enormous, enormous hawk out of the box". Macdonald uses the alliteration of "chaotic clatter" like onomatopoeia, where the sound of the word imitates the sound heard in the real world; she continues the onomatopoeia in "whirring" and "twittering". She repeats "enormous" to underline her own shock at what she is seeing.

The long sentence continues from line 16. Macdonald uses a very odd image: "in a strange coincidence of world and deed a great flood of sunlight drenches us". By "coincidence of world and deed" she means that, by chance, the sun has come out at the very moment the hawk has been released. The imagery of water in "flood" and "drenches" echoes the use of "irrigating" we noticed a few lines earlier; Macdonald is using the violent water imagery to stress how overwhelming is the sight of the hawk to her – like a flood she is carried away by what she sees, unable to resist looking at the hawk. The sentence ends with two powerful abstract nouns: "everything is brilliance and fury". Not only is there another image of light here, but one of emotion – fury, or extreme, intense and violent anger.

The next sentence lacks a main verb, and can be divided into three parts or clauses; it describes the appearance of the hawk, finally free of its box. The first section again uses alliteration on a "b" sound to mimic the dull swish of the bird's movement: "The hawk's wings, barred and beating". The next clause describes "the sharp fingers of her dark-tipped primaries cutting the air". The word "primaries" means the hawk's main flight feathers. Finally the sentence ends with "her feathers raised like the scattered quills of a fretful porpentine", which uses the simile of another animal to express the exact shape her wings are making, and the nervousness that the hawk is showing. A porpentine is an old spelling for a porcupine, which has long, thin quills as protection. Having no main verb in this sentence – just a series of present participles – makes the reader pause, as the narrative has stopped moving forward in time to focus on the appearance of the hawk.

Indeed Macdonald dispenses with verbs almost entirely between lines 19 and 23. The next sentence only has three words: "Two enormous eyes". The effect upon Macdonald is overwhelming and violent: "My heart jumps sideways" (line 20). Macdonald then gives a list of images, as she tries to express what she sees. The hawk is unreal: "She is a conjuring trick". Then come sentences without verbs: "A reptile. A fallen angel. A griffon from the pages of an illuminated bestiary".

Again we should pause here to understand what is happening. The hawk is like a reptile – this is because she seems so unlike any other bird, she is more like another creature entirely, a more threatening and strange one. The "fallen angel" is Lucifer, who is banished from heaven for pride and opposing God. This implies that the hawk is an unreal, unearthly creature, with a potential for great evil alongside great beauty. The "griffon" (more usually spelt "griffin") is a creature half-lion, half-eagle, from ancient Greek and Egyptian mythology. The creature is described as being from the pages of a medieval manuscript or "bestiary", which collected writings on a range of beasts, both real and imaginary. Again Macdonald is implying that the goshawk is far beyond other everyday creatures in ferocity and magnificence.

Macdonald then moves onto nature imagery and picks up her earlier use of water metaphors: "Something bright and distant, like gold falling through water". Macdonald is trying to get us to understand the terrible beauty and strangeness of the bird. However, she then moves quickly to try and make us understand the terrible fragility of the goshawk: "A broken marionette of wings, legs and light-splashed feathers". The bird is not free, but like a broken puppet on a string dominated by man. The man holds her by leather straps on her legs, and for an "awful, long moment" the bird is upside down "like a turkey in a butcher's shop". This simile, of a dead bird hanging in a shop, ready to be eaten, makes us aware how upset Macdonald is by this sight. By talking about a dead bird, we realise that Macdonald thinks the bird is vulnerable and in danger.

The rest of this paragraph (lines 26-31) imagines what it must be like for the goshawk herself. So, we move from what Macdonald can see, to what the bird is now able to see. The bird's whole world was an aviary or birdhouse no bigger "than a living room", and then the tiny box used to transport her. After she is moved into the outside world, Macdonald cleverly uses italics to emphasise her point, and the hawk's new freedom of vision: "she can see *everything*". Again, Macdonald does not use verbs in the sentences and gives us a list. This is a skilful contrast with the same structure early in the paragraph, but now we have the hawk's view. Many tiny details are picked out. The "point source glitter on the waves, a diving cormorant a hundred yards out; pigment flakes under wax on the lines of parked cars". These are all things that the human eye can't see. Of course, Macdonald cannot know what the bird is actually seeing – but she is using her imagination here to make us try and imagine the hawk's world, in which the bird can see "far hills" and "miles and miles of sky", and the "white scraps of gulls". The paragraph ends with a final striking sentence, which uses a metaphor of printing to show that the bird's mind is like a blank page: "Everything startling and new-stamped on her entirely astonished brain".

The next paragraph returns to the past tense and is a more conventional way of narrating a story. We now focus upon the man who brought the goshawk, rather than Macdonald or the bird itself. The man was "perfectly calm" through this first encounter, probably because he had a lot of experience. He takes the hawk "in one practised movement". Macdonald uses images of security and strength. The man is "anchoring" (line 33) the hawk's back against his chest and "gripping" the bird's "scaled yellow legs in one hand". The word "anchoring" is a metaphor taken from the sea, when a ship puts down its anchor. It implies here that the man is hold the hawk so securely it is safe.

Macdonald then introduces direct speech as the man says "Let's get that hood back on". She uses the word "tautly" to describe his voice, which is an odd image, as it is very visual and usually describes how something looks, not how it sounds: by using this word, we can imagine the tension in the man's face, and indeed Macdonald tells us immediately that "There was concern in his face. It was born of care."

Macdonald again uses the technique of introducing a long sentence amongst a series of short sentences, in line 35-39, with a single sentence in which she imagines the early life of the bird and its close relationship with the man who reared it. The hawk was "hatched in an incubator" from "a frail bluish eggshell"; Macdonald continues to stress the fragile, helpless nature of the chick, as it is fed scraps of meat with tweezers by the patient handler, the chick's "new neck wobbling with the effort of keeping her head in the air". Imagining this relationship causes Macdonald to react violently, which she emphasises with a short, startling sentence after this long one: "All at once I loved this man, and fiercely" (line 39-40). In *H is for Hawk* Macdonald is looking for a hawk to raise because of her loneliness and grief after the death of her father, and in this sentence we can see how fragile Macdonald is, and how Macdonald is empathising with the goshawk.

Macdonald looks directly at the hawk, after grabbing the hood from the box. She uses alliteration in the next sentences, linking the hawk's "wild eyes" with the colour of "sun on white paper", and using the strange image of the hawk staring because the "whole world" had "fallen into them". She is trying to explain the intensity of the hawk's gaze, and the impact it has upon her.

Once more she uses a short verbless sentence, to show how time is passing with the bird unhooded: "One, two, three" (line 42). As she hoods the bird, she feels the bird's skull and imagines what is happening in its brain. Again, she uses both alliteration and onomatopoeia as she talks of an "alien brain fizzing and fusing with terror", the "f" and "z" sounds like sparking electricity.

However, after checking the paperwork Macdonald has a terrible shock, which she uses understatement to express; a very short paragraph, without any emotional verbs or images, as if she is numb: "It was the wrong bird. This was the younger one. The smaller one. This was not my hawk". This is a deliberate contrast with the imaginative and exuberant writing of the previous paragraph. Then Macdonald uses an even more striking device: a one word paragraph, in italics, as Macdonald understands what mistaking the bird means: "*Oh*" (line 48). This is not even a proper word, it is like a sigh that Macdonald is giving.

The next paragraph describes the other hawk – the one that Macdonald had originally agreed to purchase before seeing the other, younger bird. This larger, older bird is totally different: "She came out like a Victorian melodrama: a sort of madwoman in the attack." In the first simile, a melodrama is an unrealistic play, often with showing very extreme emotions. This suggests how agitated the bird is. The phrase "madwoman in the attack" is a pun on the phrase "madwoman in the attic", which refers to the Victorian novel Jane Eyre, in which Mr Rochester's first wife, suffering from mental illness, is hidden away from everyone in the attic of the house. The meaning here is that the bird is uncontrollable and dangerous, and has a potential rage and strangeness that scares Macdonald.

This old bird is "smokier and darker", and Macdonald concentrates also upon the sound. She repeats the word "twittering" to refer to the younger bird, but contrasts its noises with the "great, awful gouts of sound like a thing in pain". The word "gouts" means large drops, usually used with blood. This is a very horrible image, and is unexpected, as gouts is not a word usually used with sound, and suggests that Macdonald is frightened of the new bird.

Macdonald uses italics three times in this paragraph to heighten tension in the reader. Firstly, she tries to convince herself this is now her bird: "*This is my hawk*" (line 53). But the bird's behaviour is such that Macdonald believes there is something "blank and crazy in her stare. Some madness from a different country". The second use of italics comes then: "*This isn't my hawk*". All the details are correct, but there is no connection between Macdonald and this bird: "*But this isn't my hawk.* Slow panic". Again, this is another sentence with no main verb, which makes it stand out, as Macdonald realises with horror that she cannot take this second, more aggressive bird.

Macdonald uses reported speech to finish the paragraph, as she dramatizes her attempts to persuade the man to let her have the younger bird. She starts off very politely: "But I really liked the first one. Do you think there's any chance I could take that one instead …?" The man doesn't react and she carries on, trying to justify the swap, but she realises that she is becoming increasingly agitated, with "a desperate, crazy barrage of incoherent appeals" (line 65). The word "barrage" comes from warfare and is a violent image of coming under enemy fire.

The final paragraph hints that these appeals "persuaded" the man: or, rather, Macdonald recognises her own appearance or expression clinches the deal. Again, she uses alliteration on "w" sounds to emphasise certain words in the next paragraph, stressing how intensely odd a "tall, white-faced women with wind-wrecked hair" looked. She uses an image taken from classical Greek theatre, comparing herself to Medea, wife of Jason, famous as captain of the *Argo* and leader of the Argonauts. In the play by Euripides, Medea, driven mad by grief that her husband has left her for another woman, kills their own children to punish Jason. Macdonald, too, has been deeply affected by grief for her father's sudden death. Macdonald though is self-deprecating, and realises she looks like she is from a "seaside production of Medea", one which is more amateurish, but for that reason possibly has more pathos and reality. The last three sentences build the tension, and in this extract we are left wondering whether he does relent. Macdonald says that her "stuttered request" must have made the man realise that the choice of the right bird was "very important". But after all the noise and emotion, Macdonald skilfully concludes with a "cliff-hanger" ending: "There was a moment of total silence" (line 70).

Chinese Cinderella by Adeline Yen Mah

Biography

Adeline Yen Mah was born in 1937 in Tianjin, China. Her father was a successful businessman, and her mother an accountant. Her mother died almost immediately after her birth, and her father soon remarried a younger woman; Yen Mah was rejected by her family and endured a traumatic and abusive childhood. The family moved to Hong Kong, and Yen Mah won a play-writing competition, after which her father finally allowed her to move to England to study medicine. Her family rejected her again after she chose to move to America to set up a medical practice. The success of her first autobiography "Falling Leaves" in 1997 allowed her to devote herself to writing, and her revision of parts of this book, "Chinese Cinderella", became a world-wide bestseller. She has written many books since.

Background

"Chinese Cinderella" was published in 1999, and is subtitled "The Secret Story of an Unwanted Daughter". It narrates mainly the treatment she suffers under her stepmother Jeanne Prosperi, but there are moments of hope and kindness with her grandfather Ye Ye and Aunt Baba. The extract being studied comes from the very end of the book.

Summary

Adeline Yen Mah in this extract tells us about an incident during her schooldays. While at boarding school, waiting for the end of term, her father's chauffeur unexpectedly turns up to take her home. Yen Mah is surprised at this, because she is usually never summoned home like this, and she is full of foreboding. We learn that the family moved house without letting her know – a sign of their neglect. However, Yen Mah is let into her father's study, and he shows her a newspaper article, which tells us that Yen Mah has won a play-writing competition. Her father is delighted – because the success reflects well upon him – and he decides to allow Yen Mah to study in England. She does not have the choice of what she will study – he dictates that she study medicine – but she is nevertheless delighted because she has the opportunity to go to England.

Analysis

The passage is an extract from an autobiography, and has a number of features typical of this genre. It is written in the first person and in the past tense. Yen Mah makes the extract lively by the use of reported speech, which brings the characters to life. Also, even though the extract is set well in her past, she does not comment on her younger self's thoughts with the benefit of hindsight; it is as if everything is happening for the first time.

The first paragraph tells us about Yen Mah's state of mind at boarding school. She is worried about leaving. She uses personification in talking about her fear of the end of term: "Time went by relentlessly", as if time is a person who is acting to oppress Adeline without mercy. In only two months school will be over and she has no idea of what is planned for her.

The next paragraph again uses sinister imagery to express Yen Mah's anxiety. Although she is playing Monopoly with friends, she is not enjoying it, and she tells us that her "heart was not in it". Even the alliteration of "warm wind" – which normally would signal a positive image of a benign natural world – is more a sign of impending trouble. A radio warns of a possible typhoon or storm, which mirrors Yen Mah's mood: a potential disaster is on its way. This is an example of what is called the "pathetic fallacy", which is when the description of the natural world mirrors what a character is feeling. Here, the storm on the way is a hint that something awful might happen to Yen Mah.

The game Monopoly is also a significant metaphor: Monopoly is a board game which involves trying to defeat your opponents in business and buy up property. Later in this extract we learn that Yen Mah's father is a successful businessman, and he is only interested in Yen Mah's success because it allows him to look good to other businessmen. By mentioning Monopoly, we are reminded how different Yen Mah's goals in life are, as she loves literature and wants to escape to become a writer, rather than have a life dictated by her father and his materialistic outlook.

Finally Yen Mah uses a powerful simile to describe her worry: "the thought of leaving school throbbed at the back of my mind like a persistent toothache" (line 6). Yen Mah is comparing her concern about leaving school with a chronic physical pain. This suggests that unlike most children who look forward to the holidays, Yen Mah experiences physical discomfort at the prospect. This tells us how awful her family life must be.

In the next few paragraphs, Yen Mah uses lively dialogue. The girls are interrupted in their game by Ma-mien Valentino, who appears to be an employee of the boarding school. She is called "Mother Valentino" by Mary, one of the girls. As this is a Catholic school, we later learn, we might think that Mother Valentino is a Nun. Mary does not want Adeline to break up the game because "for once" she is winning. But when Ma-mien Valentino appears all of the girls stand up and greet her; this shows that they have very good manners.

Ma-mien Valentino scolds Yen Mah very gently about seeming to ignore her call. She is told to hurry up as "Your chauffeur is waiting to take you home" (line 13). Yen Mah's family is obviously very wealthy.

Again, Yen Mah describes how her younger self was unsettled by the thought of going home. She uses alliteration to emphasise the strength of her negative emotion. She is "Full of foreboding", and she runs down to the car "as in a nightmare, wondering who had died this time" (line 14). By using this metaphor, she is comparing her anxiety at the potential awful news to the way a person feels whilst having a terrible bad dream. The reader understands even further here how distant are relations between her and her family; she only expects contact at times of bereavement. However her father's chauffeur tells her that everyone is well.

Yen Mah asks him why she is going home but the chauffeur replies "defensively, shrugging his shoulders". We learn that this is a household where authority is obeyed without question: "They give the orders and I carry them out" (line 18).

The drive home is only "short", which is rather sad; it means that her family is not far away, and still they do not want to see her. Yen Mah uses a powerful image to express her sadness: "my heart was full of dread". This again means that she experiences a physical sensation with the anxiety at meeting her family and discovering what has gone wrong at home, much as she had when she described the thought of going home as being like a toothache . The car pulls up at an "elegant villa" halfway between the harbour and a nearby peak; the beautiful surroundings contrast with her sense of unhappiness.

The next paragraph is very short. Yen Mah asks "where are we", adding the adverb "foolishly", though as this is the first time she has seen the house, it is far from foolish, just sad that she hasn't been told that her family had moved. The chauffeur answers "rudely", asking her "Don't you know anything?" Even her family's employees are not treating her with respect, and underestimating her intelligence. It turns out that her family moved there "a few months ago" (line 24). Yen Mah tries to save face, and acts as if she knew this all along: "I had forgotten". Again, we see that Yen Mah is often speaking in ways that disguise her true emotions.

In the examples above, we can see that Yen Mah uses adverbs a lot in her writing; adverbs are used to describe verbs, or the way that people *do* things. They often end in "ly". They are similar to adjectives, which describe *nouns*, or things themselves. Using many adverbs allows Yen Mah to describe peoples' emotions in a very effective way, using very few words. So the word "foolishly" tells us how Yen Mah feels embarrassed to be ignorant of her family's move, and the chauffeur shrugging "defensively" makes us think that he has had to be careful in the way he deals with people in authority, and that working for her family is difficult. However, the fact he can talk to her "rudely" implies that Yen Mah is of little importance.

On arriving home the door is opened by Ah Gum. The word "Ah" is used as an informal title amongst family and friends, or with trusted servants, so we could think that Ah Gum also works for the Yen Mah family. When she gets in, there is no-one to greet her. Her mother (or stepmother) is out playing bridge, and her brothers and sister are sunbathing. The fact they are described as doing other things is another example of the way Yen Mah is neglected. She is, however, formally summoned to see her father in his room.

This request surprises Yen Mah. She can only respond with a timid question: "See me in his room?" She is "overwhelmed". The imagery becomes very religious here, with an allusion to Judaism or Old Testament Christianity. She says she has been "summoned by Father to enter the Holy of Holies" (lines 31-32). The Holy of Holies was, in the Christian Old Testament or the Jewish Torah, the veiled inner sanctuary in the tabernacle, later the Temple in Jerusalem, where God dwelt, along with the Ark of the Covenant containing the Ten Commandments. Only anointed priests could enter. The use of such imagery conveys the magnitude of what Yen Mah feels she is being asked to do; her Father, like God, is to her all-powerful and his room is private and deeply secret. To be admitted is frightening, and she asks a one-word question: "Why?" (line 32).

Yen Mah starts the paragraph where she meets her father with another adverb, placed at the start of the sentence to increase its effect: "Timidly, I knocked on the door". This has very effectively established that she is scared. Yen Mah's father appears to be very conventional and harmless, and there is nothing about his appearances that is threatening to the reader. He is in slippers, bathrobe, reading a newspaper, he smiles as Yen Mah entered and is "in a happy mood". But Yen Mah is still very wary of him. She expresses this wariness in two unanswered questions which finish the paragraph: "Is this a giant ruse on his part to trick me? Dare I let my guard down?"

Her father's first words are commands: "Sit down! Sit down!" He carries on using the imperative or commanding form of the verb: "Don't look so scared". Using the imperative form of the verb shows that he is used to telling people what to do, and being obeyed.

He passes the paper to Yen Mah and tells her: "They're writing about someone we both know, I think". This is deliberately mysterious, and the truth is only revealed in the next paragraph, when young Adeline sees her name "ADELINE YEN" in capital letters.

The next paragraph is a lengthy quotation from the newspaper, and we learn more details about Adeline's life. She is fourteen and at Catholic School, and has won first prize in an international play writing competition held in London in 1952. It is the first time a Chinese student from Hong Kong has won, and Adeline has won £50 (a very large sum in 1952). The newspaper does not remain objective, though, and sees this as a matter of national pride: "Our sincere congratulations, ADELINE YEN, for bringing honour to Hong Kong. We are proud of you".

Again, Yen Mah follows this paragraph with more questions. She cannot believe that she is the winner: "Is it possible? Am I dreaming? Me the winner?" This use of a metaphor echoes the "nightmare" of earlier (line 14) when Yen Mah arrived at the house. By wondering whether she is dreaming, we can see that Yen Mah cannot believe she has won something, she thinks it must not be true. This shows us that Yen Mah has had very little success or encouragement in her life.

The rest of the extract is composed of dialogue, interspersed with Yen Mah's reactions to what her father is saying. Lines 50-54 are solely her father. He tells her that his friend C.Y. Tung, a fellow businessman, points out the article and asks whether Adeline is related to him, as the last name is uncommon. Adeline's father is delighted that Adeline has won, but not happy for her, simply happy that her achievements reflect well upon him. C.Y. Tung has a few children Adeline's age "but so far none of them has won an international literary prize". Her father goes as far to say "I was quite pleased to tell him that you are my daughter". This is very faint praise.

However, Yen Mah notes that "He looked radiant", because she "had given him face" in front of a prominent colleague. The image of having "face" means to have status in the eyes of others. A common expression related to this is "to lose face", which means to be embarrassed or belittled, causing others to lose respect. We can see that Yen Mah's father is only concerned by external appearances, rather than Yen Mah's inner happiness or satisfaction. The word "radiant" means to shine or to glow, and this shows us that Yan Mah's father is very satisfied indeed, to such an extent that it can be seen in his expression.

Again, Yen Mah asks herself a question "Is this big moment I have been waiting for?" The imagery she uses to describe her happiness is in stark contrast with the understated and grudging praise from her father: "My whole being vibrated with all the joy in the world. I only had to stretch out my hand to reach the stars" (lines 52-53). Yen Mah uses hyperbole here to describe the extent of her happiness. She feels "all the joy in the world", and the word "vibrated", which means to be shaken strongly, expresses how physical an effect the feeling of happiness has. She feels that her joy is so great she could reach out and touch the stars; the vastness of this feeling contrasts with how small she has been made to feel by her family.

Her father continues to belittle her achievement: "How come *you* won"? The word "you" is in italics to show that her father is stressing it; the implication is that Yen Mah, of all people, could never succeed, and something must be wrong. We can see here how her father has always tried to make her feel small. Yen Mah knows she has to show humility: it is what her father will expect of her. She underplays her achievements and says perhaps no-one else applied because of the complicated rules. Her father laughs "approvingly" at this show of humility and tells her that is a "good answer".

At this point, young Adeline suddenly makes her move, and Yen Mah uses another adverb skilfully to show what Yen Mah is feeling. She asks her father "boldly" whether she can go to University in England like her brothers. The word "boldly" is an antonym or opposite to the word "timidly" which we saw before; this deliberate contrast shows that Yen Mah is gaining in confidence, and had reserves of strength we might not have realised. Somewhat surprisingly, given his attitude, her father seems to agree that she has "potential", but he want to know what she plans to study.

Yen Mah is overwhelmed by the chance she will be able to go to England. Her heart "gave a giant lurch" and she realises she can go. Again, Yen Mah uses a metaphor of physical movement, her emotion is so great it is as if her heart moves violently. This tells us she has very powerful feelings, even though she cannot express them overtly.

But what is she going to do? She had not thought that far ahead. Again, she uses a question to express her state of mind: "Going to England is like entering heaven. Does it matter what you do after you get to heaven?" The use of the simile here – that England is like heaven or paradise – shows us that she feels her current life is unhappy, more like hell than heaven.

Yen Mah can only think of creative writing as a career, as she's just won a competition, and she proposes this to her father. Her father very strongly contradicts this. He "scoffs" at her idea, and says she's going to starve as a writer. Neither her Chinese nor her English will be good enough for her to be able to make a living. Yen Mah does not respond to this: "I waited in silence. I did not wish to contradict him".

Her father's final speech is mainly in the future tense: as if he is going to be able to control all aspects of her future life. He tells her "You will go to England with Third Brother this summer and you will go to medical school". She will, in her father's plan, specialise in obstetrics and deliver children. Obstetrics is the medical specialisation of delivering babies; this shows that her father only thinks women can be doctors if they are in a field that is related to childbirth. This will be a "foolproof profession" for her, which is another hidden criticism, and implies he thinks she is a fool. Her father's final question – "Don't you agree?" is a rhetorical question, which means that he is not expecting an answer. He does not expect any dissent from her.

Yen Mah's reaction is very intense, but she doesn't show it at all to her father. In her mind, she can think only of the poet William Wordsworth's famous line about the French Revolution of 1789: "*Bliss it was that dawn to be alive*". The word "bliss" means great joy; the allusion to the youthful poet's enthusiasm alerts us to the strength of Yen Mah's reaction; moving to England will be a revolution in her life, no matter what she studies, as it will bring freedom from the restrictions of her family life. But Yen Mah keeps all of this reaction secret, and complies with the role of the dutiful daughter: "Father, I shall go to medical school in England and become a doctor. Thank you very, very, very much". The only hint of her joy is in the repetition of "very" in this last line.

Throughout this extract, Yen Mah constantly asks questions, either to others, such as the chauffeur, or more commonly, to herself. These questions to herself are unspoken questions, and reflect her state of mind. They often show how nervous and anxious she is, such as the following, when her father is being unexpectedly kind: "Is this a giant ruse on his part to trick me? Dare I let my guard down?" (lines 36-37). This is a clever way of showing that Yen Mah is very wary, badly affected by constant neglect, and she questions everything that is happening to her. This very defensive and nervous way of behaving contrasts strongly with the very imaginative metaphors she uses to express her joy when she realises she has potential, such as her feeling that she could "stretch out" her hand "to reach the stars". We can see that in spite of her silent, humble exterior, Yen Mah has a very powerful imagination and strong spirit, waiting to be revealed once she leaves for England and escapes her family. Where once she could only approach life "timidly", she can now act "boldly".

Made in the USA
Lexington, KY
17 December 2017